TREASURED TIME
with your TODDLER

A MONTHLY GUIDE TO ACTIVITIES

TREASURED TIME
with your TODDLER

Jan Brennan

August House Publishers, Inc.
LITTLE ROCK

Printed in the United States of America

10 9 8 7 6 5 4 3

LIBRARY OF CONGRESS CATALOGING-IN-PUBLICATION DATA

Brennan, Jan, 1952–
Treasured time with your toddler / by Jan Brennan — 1st ed.
p.   cm.
Includes index.
ISBN 0-87483-127-X (alk. paper) : $12.95
1. Family recreation—United States. 2. Creative activities and
seat work. 3. Toddlers—United States—Recreation. I. Title.
GV1828.B744 1991
649'.5—dc20   91-15747

First Edition, 1991

Executive: Liz Parkhurst
Project editor: Judith Faust
Design director: Ted Parkhurst
Cover and illustrations: Kitty Harvill
Typography: Lettergraphics, Little Rock

This book is printed on archival-quality paper which meets
the guidelines for performance and durability of the
Committee on Production Guidelines for Book Longevity
of the Council on Library Resources.

AUGUST HOUSE, INC.   PUBLISHERS   LITTLE ROCK

To you, for caring enough
to share your time and energy
with the little treasures in your life.

Acknowledgments

I wish to thank...
...my husband, Lee, and our friend Mac for their editing,
their perfectionism, and their quality control
...my three sons—Michael, Matthew, and Kyle—
for their love, laughter, and energy
...my dear friends at the Farmington Library, especially
Nancy DeSalvo, Jane Farley, Peter Guglietta,
and Patricia Morgen,
for their professional assistance
...and my loving family and wonderful friends for
their unending support and encouragement.

CONTENTS

Preface

Anyone who has ever experienced a toddler knows that between the ages of two and three, children go through incredible changes, swinging from pleasant and loving to demanding and frustrating. One day a toddler may be all smiles, helpful, and aiming to please, while the very next day that same child may be whiny, helpless, and looking for trouble! Sometimes the only consolation is to know that it is normal behavior and that the child will eventually grow out of it.

Toddlers are incredibly energetic little people. They are so full of energy, they could play twenty-four hours a day. They love to explore their surroundings and everything within their growing reach. Play to them is more than mere play—it is a valuable learning process through which the child investigates the world in which he or she lives. The more a toddler discovers and learns, the more independent he feels; an important pride in self begins to grow. He needs to be given opportunities to do things by himself as this independence becomes a major focus in his life.

At the same time she is demanding independence, the toddler desperately needs routines and boundaries within which to live. Routines help set the limits that ease her mind. Bedtime routines, saying-goodbye routines, mealtime routines—all firmly and lovingly enforced—help keep things in order.

Not only do toddlers change dramatically from day to day, but one toddler's abilities may be quite different from those of another. While one two year old might be able to recite his alphabet, count to fifty, and identify every shape and color, another three year old may only know red, yellow, and blue. Every child will learn in his own good time, and parents should merely set the stage for learning to take place—and then relax and let it happen when the time is right.

Reading is one of the most important things to do with a toddler. Not only does it afford special time together but it also opens his eyes to new worlds, imaginary and real, through the magic of pictures and words.

Toddlerhood is a time of great changes and learning for the child, and one that requires great patience and understanding from the adult. *Treasured Time With Your Toddler* offers easy, positive ways to help both adult and child get the most out of this stage in a child's life.

The book is organized into months and weeks, and each weekly chapter includes book suggestions, recipes, verses to recite or songs to sing, and activities. Each week has a theme borrowed from a nursery rhyme or song, primarily Mother Goose rhymes.

Children today are still introduced to the world of literature by Mother Goose.

Through rhythmic and rhyming verses like "Jack and Jill" and "Wee Willie Winkie," children learn to play with the sounds of language. Through action verses and refrains like "London Bridge" and "Baa Baa Black Sheep," children participate in simple language games. Through short-story verses like "Little Miss Muffet" and "Humpty Dumpty," children experience full stories with action, climax, and ending. Through humorous verses like "Dr. Foster" and riddle verses like "Teeth and Gums," children learn the subtleties of humor. There are few other sources that offer so much with such perfect simplicity as children's literature.

Children's literature is a wonderful foundation on which to base a child's entire education. Using a simple verse or a story as a springboard, all kinds of follow-up learning can take place. Children are learning valuable lessons while they're being enchanted and delighted by Mother Goose.

It is my hope that through the use of this book, your days, too, will be more enchanting and delightful as you spend some treasured time with your toddler

List of Materials

Throughout this book, activities are suggested that use materials you would be likely to have on hand at home. Below is a list of items most often called for, some of which you may want to start saving.

balloons
brown packaging paper
brown paper bags, grocery size and lunch size
bubbles
buttons
chalk
clear contact paper
construction paper, all colors
cotton
cottonballs
crayons
crepe paper streamers
egg cartons
empty boxes of all sizes
facial tissues
finger paint
glitter
glue
marking pens, broad-tipped
masking tape
oaktag (poster board)

old magazines, catalogs, and cards
old photos
old socks
paper clips
paper towels
peanuts in shells
popsicle sticks
ribbon
rubber bands
sandpaper
scissors, child safety
scrap material, including carpet, canvas, corrugated cardboard, fabric, etc.
soap
sponges
straws
string
tempera paint
tissue paper
toothpicks
yarn

Chapter One

JANUARY

Wintertime Treasures

Winter weather can mean different things for you and your child depending on where you live. If you live where snows blow and days are invigorating and cold, it can mean plenty of outdoor playtime— frolicking in the snow, sledding, building snowmen. If you live where winter temperatures dip only slightly from the rest of the year, your time outdoors may be spent frolicking in the sunshine, swimming, and building pretend snowmen out of materials other than snow. Whether your January days are snowy or warm, you'll find winter fun activities in this chapter that will be appropriate for you.

Of course, there are always winter days, no matter where you live, when the weather is just too nasty to go outside. You'll find lots of indoor play opportunities suggested in this chapter as well.

The last week of this month's activities deals with an almost inevitable byproduct of winter: getting sick. Viruses and flu seem to love the winter season as much as your little one does, so be prepared to cheer up your achy, feverish child.

Winter treasures for your time with your toddler are waiting to be found in this January chapter. Read on and pick out your favorites to do with your little treasure.

FIRST WEEK

Play Days

How many days has my baby to play?
Saturday, Sunday, Monday,
Tuesday, Wednesday, Thursday,
Friday,
Saturday, Sunday, Monday.

The importance of play must not be underestimated, for it is through play that a child learns. He learns about the real world by exploring his environment and using his five senses. He learns how to be creative and imaginative through make-believe play. He learns how to express his feelings by trying out countless situations in play. He learns how to use his physical body through free play and manipulating toys.

There is so much we as parents can do to enhance our children's play. First of all, we should play with them and support their ideas and interests. Second, we should plan ahead to have appropriate materials on hand to encourage and augment their play. And lastly, we should enter their imaginary world and enjoy it. Two and three year olds still need a great deal of guidance and interaction with their play, and even if sometimes you feel like you're wasting your time "just playing," you aren't. Think about all the valuable lessons your child is learning and about how you're strengthening the bond between you as you play together, and then relax. These precious play times will be gone all too soon. Make the most of them, for your child and for yourself.

READINGS

How Many Days Has Baby to Play? by Joan Walsh Anglund (Harcourt Brace Jovanovich)

A little child plays her way through the week with her friend, the bear. Ms. Anglund's characters and sweet illustrations show many different play situations.

Playtime by Cynthia Mitchell (Collins World)

This simply written, beautifully illustrated book shows children hard at work—playing in every situation imaginable! Children do indeed learn about life as they play, and this book depicts that very clearly.

Each Peach Pear Plum by Janet and Allan Ahlberg (The Viking Press; pb Penguin)

In this 'I Spy' book, the reader follows familiar Mother Goose verses and is asked to find various Mother Goose characters cleverly hidden in the illustrations.

William the Vehicle King by Laura P. Newton (Bradbury Press)

William gets so involved in playing with his cars and trucks and other vehicles that his room turns into a busy intersection filled with fun and action. Any child who loves to play with cars will enjoy this lively book.

RECITINGS

I LOVE TO PLAY
(Sung to "Jingle Bells")

Dashing through the house
Looking for something to play,
I grab my Daddy's hand,
Laughing all the way.

We run downstairs to see
What's there for him and me.
We grab some books right on the shelf
And sit right down to read.

Chorus:

I love to play, every day,
With Mom and Dad and friends.
We have such fun, it's never done,
We never let it end.
We play by day, we play by night,
We play whenever we can.
Playing is a part of life,
That I never want to end!

Dashing through the house
Looking for something to play,
I grab my Mommy's hand,
Laughing all the way.

We run outside to see
What's there for her and me,
Swings and balls and bats and trikes,
To keep us company.

Chorus

Dashing through the house
Looking for something to play,
I grab my best friend's hand,
Laughing all the way.

We run around to see,
What's there for her *(or him)* and me,
Crayons and paper, paints and more
To make something pretty.

Chorus

DRESSING UP
(Sung to "Yankee Doodle")

(Michael Brennan) walked around,
Dressed up just like a fireman,
He wore big boots, a fireman's hat,
And rang the bell with both hands.

Chorus:

Dressing up is lots of fun,
Try it and you'll see.
Teachers, policemen, astronauts,
Who would you like to be?

(Michael Brennan) walked around,
Dressed up just like a circus clown,
He had a smile a mile wide,
And the biggest nose around town.

Chorus

Make up more verses according to your child's requests. You may wish to suggest animals, characters from favorite stories, or other kinds of people for your child to dress up like.

SONGS: There are many excellent children's records that have wonderful activities for

children and adults to enjoy together. Several are listed below:

Activity Songs to Grow On by Marcia Berman, Scholastic Records

Children's Creative Play Songs Volume I by Teddy Bear Records, Stepping Tones Records

It's Toddler Time by Carol Hammett, Kimbo Educational Records

Music for 1's and 2's by Tom Glazer, CMS Records

Nursery Rhymes—Rhyming and Remembering by Ella Jenkins, Folkways Records

Singable Songs for the Very Young by Raffi, Shoreline Records

Songs to Grow On by Woody Guthrie, Folkways Records

Tickly Toddle by Hap Palmer, Educational Activities Records

Don't overlook the simple ones you have known since you were a child. Songs like "Ring Around the Rosie" are loved for their rhythm as well as their action. Hold hands, walk around in a circle and fall down at the end.

> Ring around the rosie,
> A pocket full of posies.
> Ashes, ashes,
> We all fall down!

RECIPES

These two easy recipes are fun in several ways. For one thing, your little one can help prepare them by stirring, mixing, adding ingredients, or whatever's appropriate for your particular child. For another, the two recipes can be used as art mediums! And finally, they are deliciously edible, so if you have a child who still puts things in his mouth, these are perfect art projects for him!

PEANUT BUTTER PLAY CLAY

1. Mix together 1 cup of peanut butter, 3 tablespoons of honey, and approximately 1 cup of nonfat dry milk powder. Mix well.

2. Hand out as much playdough as your child can handle and begin manipulating it in various ways. Show your child different things he can do, such as rolling it into a ball, squashing the ball with his palm, poking holes in the dough with his fingers, using cookie cutters to make shapes, etc. Then let him experiment.

Do this activity *after* lunch when your child is already full so he won't eat too much, or incorporate it into his lunch and let him eat as much as he wishes, accompanied with milk, crackers, fruit, and other foods to round off the meal. It is near impossible to expect a child not to enjoy eating this delicious play clay!

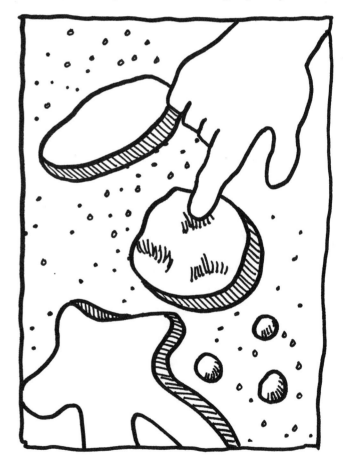

FINGER–PAINT PUDDING

Mix up a box of packaged pudding or make your own favorite recipe (one offered below). Pour it out on a cookie sheet, and let your child finger paint with a paint she can eat!

1. Blend ½ cup sugar, ⅓ cup cocoa or carob, 2 tablespoons cornstarch, and ⅛ teaspoon salt in a two-quart pan.

2. Combine 2 cups milk and 2 egg yolks, slightly beaten.

3. Gradually stir milk mixture into sugar mixture.

4. Cook over medium heat, stirring constantly until mixture thickens and boils; then boil about 1 minute.

5. Remove from heat; stir in 2 teaspoons vanilla.

6. Cool and chill.

ACTIVITIES

IMITATION

Children love to imitate their parents. Your work is their play. Give your child various "jobs" to do that will be easy enough for him to successfully accomplish and give him a feeling of pride. Putting away folded clothes, loading some of the utensils into the dishwasher, stirring and measuring ingredients in cooking, and putting cans, glass, plastics, and paper in the recycling container are some that twos and threes can successfully handle.

TOGETHERCISE

There are many benefits from exercising, and children can reap these benefits, too. Not only will they love the "workout," they will enjoy the contact with you as you do various routines together. Here are a few exercises that work well.

■ You lie down on the floor and have your child sit gently on your stomach. As you sit up, hold her hands and have her lie down. As you pull her up to a sitting position, you lie back down. This "see-saw" sit-up is fun and a good stomach exercise—but remember to keep your stomach tight throughout the exercise.

■ Lie on your back with your knees tucked up to your chest. Have your child lie on top of your knees and lower legs and wrap his arms around the back of your lower legs. With him holding on tightly, raise your legs and extend them as far as you can safely. These leg raises are great for your quadriceps and are a thrill for your child.

There are many other exercises you can do together. Experiment and have fun.

TOGETHER WALK

Go for a walk together—either indoors or outdoors—and collect things that you can later use in art projects. Some examples of things to gather: indoors—junk mail, string, yarn, scrap material, old cards; outdoors—pebbles, twigs, leaves, pinecones, seeds, nuts. Keep your collections in bags for days when you wish to do some cutting and gluing.

When that time has arrived, using child-safe scissors, and being sure to supervise carefully, let your child cut and make patterns with your nature materials, and then glue his artwork on oaktag, cardboard or construction paper.

Be there to offer assistance, but don't interfere with the actual artwork, as she should be allowed to "do her own thing".

SECOND WEEK

Tell Me A Story

I'll tell you a story
About Jack-a-Nory:
And now my story's begun.
I'll tell you another
About his brother:
And now my story is done.

You've heard many times that one of the most important things you can do with your child is to read with her. Why? What is so special about reading with your child?

To begin with, when you read with your child, you're sharing some special time together that makes the bond between the two of you even stronger. Solving mysteries, conquering fears, or laughing at comical situations while you sit close together on the couch increases your shared experiences and deepens your relationship and your love.

Reading opens your child's eyes to a world as wide and vast as the imagination. You will introduce her to thousands of new characters, situations, places and experiences. Her attention span will increase, her imagination will be stimulated, her memory skills will be sharpened, her understanding of others will expand, her life will be enriched. Not bad when you consider that all this can happen in as little as ten minutes a day!

Set aside a little slice of time each day to share this wonderful gift with your child as you read with her and open up her world.

READINGS

Sam Who Never Forgets by Eve Rice (Penguin; pb Morrow)

Sam is a zoo keeper who feeds all the animals. One day, it appears that Sam forgot to feed Elephant, and all the animals are sad for Elephant. But Sam hasn't forgotten—and the reader won't forget the poignant message in this book. This is a very reassuring book for little ones.

Even If I Did Something Awful by Barbara S. Hazen (Macmillan)

At one time or another, every child wonders if his mom or dad still love him—especially after he has done something bad. This is a story about a little girl who questions her mom about this very thing and gets a realistic, honest, and loving answer. This is another reassuring book that is a treasure to share.

Beady Bear by Don Freeman (Penguin; pb Penguin)

Beady Bear is a wind-up bear who belongs to a little boy named Thayer. They are best friends. One day, Beady reads in a book that bears live in caves, so he sets out to find a cave to live in. It is then that both he and Thayer realize how much they need each other. The story is written in rhyme

Corduroy by Don Freeman (Penguin; pb Penguin)

Corduroy is a small bear who wants to be loved by someone. When he is bought by a little girl named Lisa, he knows what happiness really is.

18

RECITINGS

LOVE AND MAGIC

Do you know Sam?
He was the zoo man
Who gave all the animals their food.

And do you know Corduroy?
He is a little bear boy
Whose life turned out to be so good.

Leo the Late Bloomer,
There was a rumor,
Couldn't do anything right.

While Beady Bear
Was afraid no one cared
When he was alone one night.

Stories new and old
Are waiting to be told
Where charming new friends abound.

Pick out a new book
And take a look:
There is love and magic to be found.

TELL ME A STORY, DADDY

Tell me a story, Daddy,
A story to make me smile.
Introduce me to some new book friends,
And we'll sing and play for awhile.

Tell me a story, Daddy,
A story that's all pretend.
Monsters, no matter how ugly and mean,
Go away at the story's end.

Tell me a story, Daddy,
A story that will really move—
Speeding trains and soaring planes
And vehicles that are ever so smooth.

Tell me a story, Daddy,
Any story will do.
For I love to sit in your lap
And spend time alone with you.

RECIPES

SAM'S CORNY BANANA OAT BREAD

Sam, in **Sam Who Never Forgets**, feeds some of his animals oats, some corn, and some bananas. Combine them all into this delicious bread to share with your little one.

1. Preheat oven to 350°.

2. Cream together ½ cup margarine and ¼ cup brown sugar.

3. Add 2 eggs.

4. Combine 1 cup whole-wheat flour, ½ cup cornmeal, ½ cup rolled oats, ¼ cup wheat germ, 1 teaspoon baking soda, and ¼ teaspoon salt. Add this mixture to the margarine mixture alternately with 1 cup mashed bananas (2–3 medium).

5. Bake in greased 9" x 5" loaf pan for 1 hour.

TELL–ME–A–STORY CAKE

After reading one of your child's favorite stories, celebrate with a special cake you can decorate together.

Bake whatever cake you'd like, whether from a cake mix or a favorite recipe. Bake it in two 8- or 9-inch layer pans. While it is baking, prepare a frosting and the following decorations.

■ Melt 6 ounces of semisweet chocolate pieces and 1 tablespoon of margarine in a double boiler. Cover a baking sheet with waxed paper and spread the chocolate mixture ⅛ inch thick on the baking sheet. Chill until firm.

■ Use a cookie cutter (or draw an outline of the shape) that will represent the character from the story that you just read with your child. For example, if you just read *Beady Bear* or *Corduroy,* use a cookie cutter of a bear. When the chocolate is hard, carefully press down with the cookie cutter to cut out the figures. Use them to decorate the frosted cake and celebrate the story with your child.

ACTIVITIES

STORY DRAMATICS

Using a story that you and your child especially enjoy, do a little creative dramatics with it. Perhaps you can take turns being some of the characters from the story and interacting with each other as those characters. For example, Corduroy and Lisa might go for a drive to see Grandpa—you and your child can take turns "driving." You may wish to make up some new stories with the characters from a book you both love. You can get as elaborate as you wish with this drama—perhaps adding drawings or puppets or background music.

SIMPLE BOARD GAME

Make up a simple game board that can go along with one of your favorite books. Use a large piece of poster board. Begin by drawing a winding path of squares that will lead from the starting gate to the ending goal. (For example, if you are following the story of **Sam Who Never Forgets**, the starting point can be at the first cage of animals that Sam fed, have the path wind around the other cages, then lead over to Elephant's cage.) Color each square red, blue, green, or yellow. Add illustrations as seem appropriate. Play the game by taking turns rolling a color die or spinning a homemade color spinner and moving to the color space indicated on the die or spinner. Make the game very short for little ones. Perhaps two or three rolls or spins will bring her to the end. For older children, add some pitfalls and "move back" spaces to add to the challenge.

ORIGINAL SONGS

Make up a song that can go along with a story you and your child have made up. Use a familiar tune like "Three Blind Mice," *"Frère Jacques,"* or "Row, Row, Row Your Boat" and add your own lyrics.

THIRD WEEK

Winter

January brings the snow
Makes our feet and fingers glow.

The winter season offers many appealing and exciting things to do both outdoors when the weather permits and indoors when the weather doesn't. Read on to see if you might find some new treasures of special things to do with your child this wintertime.

READINGS

Winter Days by Harold Roth (Grosset & Dunlap)

This board book shows young readers many winter treats both indoors and out. It is part of a series called "Babies Love Photo Board Books."

Happy Winter by Karen Gundersheimer (Harper & Row Junior Books; pb Harper & Row Junior Books)

This book is filled with lovely ideas and illustrations of exciting things to do in the winter time.

A Winter Day by Douglas Florian (Greenwillow Books)

Douglas Florian uses gentle pictures and simple text to show a child's perfect winter day.

RECITINGS

SING A SONG OF WINTER
(Sung to "Sing a Song of Sixpence")

Sing a song of winter,
Of snowflakes in the air,
Catch them as they float down
And land everywhere.

Catch one on your mitten,
Catch one on your nose,
Catch one on your tongue,
To taste this winter's snow.

Sing a song of winter,
Of yards filled up with snow.
Sledding fun is special,
Whatever speed you go.

Sing a song of winter,
Such fun in many ways.
Don't you wish this winter fun
Could last for many days?

WINTER TIME
(Sung to "Mary Had a Little Lamb")

Winter time brings outdoor fun,
Outdoor fun, outdoor fun,
Winter time brings outdoor fun,
With sun and snow and ice.

We'll take our sleds and ride down hills,
Ride down hills, ride down hills,
We'll take our sleds and ride down hills,
Won't it be so nice!

And winter time brings indoor fun,
Indoor fun, indoor fun,
Winter time brings indoor fun,
With books, crayons, games and toys.

We'll read and play the whole day long,
Whole day long, whole day long,
We'll read and play the whole day long,
We'll be happy girls and boys.

RECIPES

Have a little "Tea Party," either when you've come in from an invigorating play time outdoors or to break up a long indoor play period.

Make the following mini-muffins and fruit tea and serve them with your toddler's favorite tea set or fancy paper plates that your child can personally design.

MINI-MUFFINS

1. Preheat oven to 425°.

2. Mix the following ingredients till well-combined: 1 cup flour, ½ teaspoon baking powder, ½ cup sugar, ½ cup milk, ⅓ cup oil, 1 egg, 1 teaspoon vanilla, and 1 teaspoon lemon peel.

3. Fill greased mini-muffin tins half full.

4. Choose one of the following toppings to add before baking: (1) 1 tablespoon sugar mixed with ½ teaspoon lemon peel sprinkled on top of the batter, (2) scant teaspoon jam swirled into the top portion of the batter of each muffin, or (3) ½ cup chopped walnuts, 1 tablespoon sugar, and ¼ teaspoon cinnamon mixed together and sprinkled on top of the batter.

5. Bake at 425° for 14 minutes. Makes 24 mini-muffins—or 12 regular muffins, if you prefer.

ORANGE TEA

1. Mix equal portions of cranberry juice and orange juice.

2. Prepare one orange for each person in the following way: cut a very thin slice off the bottom (so the orange will stand up, but still serve as a cup), cut open the top and scoop out the pulp.

3. Mash the pulp very fine if you wish to add it to the drink, and then heat the drink in a saucepan. When it's warm, pour the "tea" into each orange cup and sip with a straw.

ACTIVITIES

OUTDOOR WINTER FUN

Sledding is one of the most popular winter activities when there is snow on the ground. Either pull your child around the yard on a sled to which you've attached a rope, go sledding down some hills together if your child wants you to be right there with her, or take her to a hill that she can sled on her own.

Other games that you can play outdoors include: follow the leader (making sure the leader makes fun and varied tracks in the snow for the followers to follow); tracking—looking for animal tracks that might be seen on the snow; making and following mazes made in the snow (take a shovel and make your own maze as easy or as difficult as you'd like).

Those of you who live in snowless climates might try some of these activities in the mud or sand.

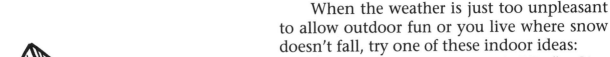

INDOOR WINTER FUN

When the weather is just too unpleasant to allow outdoor fun or you live where snow doesn't fall, try one of these indoor ideas:

■ Play: "Do As I Say, Not As I Do"—Give verbal commands to your child to do something as you physically do something else. For example: as you are scratching your right arm, say, "Scratch your foot". This is not only fun and silly, but encourages your child to really listen.

■ Box Fun—Take out as many boxes you can find in your house, and let your child's imagination take over. You might have some oatmeal boxes, shoe boxes, leftover Christmas boxes, or boxes small appliances came in. They make great starting kits for an afternoon of fun. They can be building blocks, musical instruments, houses for small "creatures," hiding places, suitcases—indeed, almost anything.

INDOOR SNOW

You don't have to be outside to enjoy snow. Bring some snow inside and let your child play with it. Some things you might wish to try: spoon it, chop it, stir it, watch how long it will take for it to melt, watch what happens when you put it in water, make snowballs, make miniature snowmen or other designs with it. As you and your child play, you'll probably come up with more.

FOURTH WEEK

Snowfriends

All the hills are covered with snow,
Time to make our snowfriends grow!

January snow offers children many exciting opportunities for play, like catching snowflakes on tongues, making tracks in the snow, and racing down hills on slippery sleds. But there is something else made possible by winter snow that some little ones take to with great enthusiasm and others approach with awe and timidity. Creating and building snowfriends can be much more than the simple playtime activity it seems, especially for young children. Once the snowfriend is complete, it can be a magical friend with whom to fantasize and play. A child's vivid imagination can take him anywhere with his newly made snowfriend—an incredible educational toy, made possible by a simple snowfall! The only caution to parents of little ones is that sometimes when the snowfriend begins to melt away, there are sad and confused feelings. Reality and fantasy can intertwine and may need some tender and careful explaining. Reassure your child that all is well, and perhaps another snowfriend is waiting to be discovered as soon as the next snow blankets the world.

READINGS

It's Snowing, Little Rabbit by Marie Wabbes (Atlantic Monthly Press; pb Little Brown & Co)

Little Rabbit bundles up and rushes outside to play in the freshly fallen snow. He makes a snowball to which he keeps adding more and more snow until he ends up with a fine surprise. This book is simply written, simply illustrated, and a joy to read.

The Snowman by Jim Erskine (Crown)

Two bears enjoy building a snowman together until they each claim it as their own. After disappointments and snowball fights, they come up with a fine solution together.

Raymond Briggs' The Snowman by Raymond Briggs (Little Brown & Co.)

There are four books in The Snowman series—***Building the Snowman, Dressing Up, Walking in the Air,*** and ***The Party.*** All four are board books with pictures from the movie/video of the same name. There are no words, so your child and you can use your imaginations to create the conversation between the little boy and his snowman in these touching books.

RECITINGS

I'M A LITTLE SNOWMAN
(Sung to "I'm a Little Teapot")

I'm a little snowman,
Round and fat.
Here are my eyes,
And here is my hat.
I love to play with children,
dogs and cats,
And catch some snowflakes—just like that!

JACK AND JILL
(Sung to "Jack and Jill")

Jack and Jill went up the hill,
To make a great big snowman;
Jack began, rolled with two hands,
And shaped a great big snowman.

Jill joined in, added nose and grin,
And eyes and scarf and buttons;
When both were done, they'd had such fun,
They started all over again.

RECIPES

ICE CREAM SNOWFRIEND

1. Scoop out two scoops of vanilla ice cream, placing one on top of the other.

2. Decorate the snowfriend's face and body with nuts, raisins and other dried fruits.

3. Place a flat cookie and a marshmallow on top of the head as the snowfriend's top hat.

BANANA SNOWMEN

1. Slice a banana into 9 equal slices.

2. Slide three banana slices onto a wooden skewer, plastic stirring stick, or long toothpick to resemble a snowman.

3. Dip both sides of the banana snowman in shredded coconut, wheat germ, chopped nuts, or other coating and put the snowman on a plate. Freeze for about 2 hours. Repeat with the remaining 6 banana pieces. Makes 3 banana snowmen.

4. Help your child slide the three pieces off the skewer and arrange them on her plate before eating them. She could add eyes or other features by using raisins and nuts.

ACTIVITIES

COTTONBALL SNOWFRIEND

Draw three big chalk circles (to make the outline of a snowman) on a piece of black construction paper. Have your child glue cottonballs inside each circle to fill it up. Use white crayons or chalk to draw the arms and top hat. Cut pieces of colored paper to glue on for eyes, nose, mouth, and any other decorations your child might like on his snowfriend.

SLEEPING SNOWFRIEND

Building a snowfriend is not a simple task for a toddler, so making this "sleeping" version will be fun and more age-appropriate for your little one. Make three adjoining circles in the snow by stomping out your footprints. Have your child follow your footsteps. When the body of the snowfriend has been made, decide with your child how to add the features. Two balls could serve as the eyes, a sand scoop could be the nose, a piece of rope could be the mouth, and other outdoor small toys could be the buttons. Use your imagination and have fun with this different version of a snowfriend.

SOCK SNOWMEN

Take an old white sock and have your child stuff it with facial tissue, paper towels, scrap material or cotton. Tie it in two places to make the divisions for a snowman. Help your child add eyes, nose, mouth, and other features made of scrap materials. You might play "Hide the Snowman." Have your child hide his snowman somewhere in the room; you try to find it.

TISSUE SNOWMAN

Draw an outline of a snowman on construction paper. Give your child some white tissue paper that you have torn into small pieces. Have her crumple the paper into little balls, then glue the balls onto the snowman to fill him up. Keep in mind not to make the snowman larger than her attention span!

FIFTH WEEK

Sick

I do not like thee, Doctor Fell.
The reason why I cannot tell,
But this I know and know full well,
I do not like thee, Doctor Fell.

I sympathize with doctors. Unfortunately for them, it's true that some people don't like them because they give us bad-tasting medicine, painful shots, and news we don't want to hear. Fortunately for us, they are there to help us when we need them. No one likes being sick, and doctors understand that better than anyone else. That's why they do the things they do.

The winter season seems to bring on all kinds of colds, flu, and other illnesses. Some small sick people need a doctor's attention, others need only the tender care that a mom or dad can give. You hope your family will escape most of this year's infectious germs, but if you don't, you can be prepared to handle your downcast little one with some of these suggestions.

READINGS

Teddy Bears Cure a Cold by Susanna Gretz (Macmillan; pb Scholastic)

No one believes William when he announces he's sick until he refuses to play monkey-in-the-middle. Then each of his friends does his own thing to try to make William feel better. The reader will be surprised to see what works best to encourage William's quick return to health.

Sick in Bed by Anne and Harlow Rockwell (Macmillan)

This gentle story is about a little boy's experience with getting sick. The reader goes to the doctor's office with him, climbs in bed to rest with him, and sympathizes when he has to get a shot. Five days later, the reader also gets to celebrate with him when he feels great again.

A Visit From Dr. Katz by Ursula K. LeGuin (Macmillan)

When Marianne gets the flu and has to stay in bed, she is very sad. She gets visited by two very unusual "doctors," who speed her on the road to recovery. This is an especially soothing story for a little one to have read to him while convalescing in bed.

RECITINGS

SNEEZING AND COUGHING
(Sung to "Working on the Railroad")

I've been sneezing and a-coughing,
All the livelong day,
I've got a cold that's pretty awful,
And it just won't go away.
Can't you see my droopy eyelids?
I can't keep my eyes awake.
Can't you see my sore and red nose?
Don't I deserve a break?

Oh, I've got to blow,
Oh, I've got to blow,
Oh, I've got to blow my no-o-ose.
Oh, I've got to blow,
Oh, I've got to blow,
Oh, I've got to blow my nose.

Someone's in the kitchen, I hear you.
Someone's in the kitchen, I know.

Someone's in the kitchen, I hear you,
Making chicken soup to go.
And singing, "Drink up, drink it all up,
Drinking liquids helps a cold;
Drink up, drink it all up,
I care and want your cold to go!"

SNIFFLE, SNIFFLE
(Sung to "Twinkle, Twinkle, Little Star")

Sniffle, sniffle, little cold,
Won't you do what you were told?
Go away—leave me alone,
I don't mean to lay here and moan,
But sniffle, sniffle it's so sad
To be so sick and feel so bad.

Sniffle, sniffle, little cold,
I'm doing all that I've been told.
I'm drinking many cups of juice,
I'm resting lots and sleeping, too.
So sniffle, sniffle, it won't be long,
Till I win out, and you'll be gone.

RECIPES

TURKEY RICE SOUP

Everyone knows homemade chicken soup does wonders for the ailing. Try some of this delicious turkey rice soup, and see if it can make your little one feel better, too!

1. Fill a large pot with 8 cups of water and/or chicken broth. Bring to a boil.

2. Add leftover turkey bones with scraps of meat still on them, and simmer for 1 hour.

3. Remove the bones, leaving broth in the pot.

4. Add 1 chopped small onion, 2 or 3 stalks of diced celery, ½ cup diced carrots, ½ cup cooked rice, 2 diced raw potatoes, ½ cup peas, and several sprigs of fresh parsley. Simmer for 30 minutes. Add salt and pepper to taste.

FEEL-BETTER APPLE

If you're healthy, this apple will keep you that way. If you're sick, this apple will at least bring a smile to your face!

1. Wash and polish a fresh apple.

2. Choose some things you know the recipient especially likes with which to "decorate" the apple. They might include cheese cubes, pineapple chunks, banana chunks, grapes, dried apricots, raisins, pieces of pears, or any other foods that can be pierced.

3. Stick one end of a toothpick into each of the decorations and the other end into the apple. (It will probably look funny, but it will be tasty.)

Note: You need to supervise this so your child doesn't swallow the toothpick.

ACTIVITIES

If your sick one needs to spend some time in bed, here are some activities that can be enjoyed while your child is resting.

DRAW ME A...

Whether you're a good artist or a terrible one matters not a bit to your child. Get a pencil and a pad of paper, and ask your child what she would like you to draw for her. She'll treasure your drawings because you made them especially for her. (They might even bring a smile to her face.)

DRAW MY FACE

Have your child close his eyes. Take the eraser end of a pencil and lightly outline all of his facial features. This may tickle a little, but it will definitely relax and soothe. Focusing all

dash and a dash, and a big question mark. Tickle up, tickle down, tickle all around. This is the way to give you the chills!" Draw the various signs as you recite the pattern.

STORYTELLING

Storytelling—sometimes just the *word* "storytelling"—leaves parents feeling inadequate and frightened. Making up a story as you go along sounds so difficult, but it really isn't, if you try. Children love best those stories that involve the people they know. Whether you tell something real that happened to you as a child, something that happened to your child

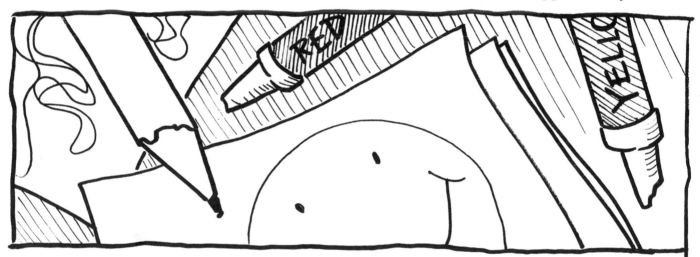

your attention on your sick child, even for a few minutes, can sometimes make all the difference in the world.

BACK DRAWING

Similar to "Draw My Face," this relaxing activity requires you to draw with your finger on your child's back. You might want to draw shapes, letters, words, pictures, or patterns. Do whatever your child would like.

One pattern that we do in our family is this: "X marks the spot to a dot and a dot. A

when he was younger (perhaps his birth), a family vacation, or a made-up story in which he is the main character, he will listen very intently and will love every word you say. Try it, and see if it's as hard as you thought.

You might also suggest that he tell you a story. If he needs something to start with, give him a character and a problem, then let his imagination take over. A younger child will need to be frequently prompted with questions.

Chapter Two

FEBRUARY

Treasures We Love

When we think of February, we think of Valentine's Day, a holiday when we celebrate love. February is a time you can focus on the meaning of love for your child and try to define it in terms she will understand.

In addition to the people your child loves, she probably loves attention focused on herself. Her birthday, for example, is important because it's truly her own special day.

At the same time your child is paying great attention to herself, she is also beginning those first attempts at declaring independence "Me do it myself!" is an often-heard expression as she experiments with being separate from mom and dad.

This struggle may be joined by another one—that of understanding where she fits into the family structure. Having to get along with other family members is not always easy, and she is beginning to deal with this situation—as are mom and dad!

In this chapter, you'll find activities for exploring love, suggestions on celebrating your little love's birthday, and ways to help your little love deal with her independence and her family.

FIRST WEEK

One I Love

One I love, two I love,
Three I love, I say;
Four I love with all my heart
And shall do from this day.

"I love you" are three of the most important words in your child's vocabulary. Whether he truly understands the phrase or is just able to say it, these three words bring a peaceful sense of security when he hears them. To a toddler, love generally centers around his immediate family. He has a strong desire—and need—to be with Mom and/or Dad. He wants to do things with Mom and/or Dad because he likes them and has fun with them. He feels happy and safe when he's with them.

If you were to ask your child what love is, he probably couldn't tell you. Perhaps he would give you a kiss or a hug to show his feelings. Love is hard for a child to explain. You can't point to it, you can't draw it (other than perhaps with a heart), and it's tough to describe in words.

With Valentine's Day this month, plan some special projects that will help your toddler understand the meaning of love. The ones offered below will get you started and may give you some ideas about how to explain love in ways your little one can understand.

READINGS

Some Things Go Together by Charlotte Zolotow (Crowell Junior Books; pb Harper & Row Junior Books)

There are certain things that just naturally go together: gardens with flowers, clocks with hours, hats with heads, and pillow with beds. The most important pair in any child's eyes is "you with me." This gentle rhyming book is a warm Valentine for a young reader.

Love is a Special Way of Feeling by Joan Walsh Anglund (Harcourt)

Love is "the safe way we feel when we sit on our mother's lap with her arms around us tight and close." This poignant description of love—and the many others in the book—help children of all ages identify and speak their feelings of love.

Just For You by Mercer Mayer (Western Publishing Co; pb Western Publishing Co)

One of Mercer Mayer's adorable little "critters" wants to do something very special for his mommy to show how much he loves her, but everything he tries turns out differently than he had planned. He does, though, come up with the perfect thing in the end.

RECITINGS

LOVE, LOVE
(Sung to "Rain, Rain")

Love, love, what is love?
A feeling kind and caring,
Enjoying spending time together,
Happy to be sharing.

Love, love, what is love?
Love is warm and tender,
Knowing you won't be alone,
True love lasts forever.

LOVE TO YOU
(Sung to "Skip To My Lou")

Love, love, love to you,
Love, love, love to you,
Love, love, love to you,
Love to you, my darling.

I love being with you, yes I do,
I love being with you, yes I do,
I love being with you, yes I do,
Love to you, my darling.

We play well together, yes it's true,
We play well together, yes it's true,
We play well together, yes it's true,
Love to you, my darling.

We'll be friends forever, me and you,
We'll be friends forever, me and you,
We'll be friends forever, me and you,
Love to you, my darling.

RECIPES

VALENTINE'S DAY LUNCH

1. Make your child's favorite sandwich; cut it with a heart-shaped cookie cutter or cut it into a heart shape with a knife. (If your child likes peanut butter and jelly, use a red jelly.)
2. Serve a red juice, such as cranberry or cranberry-apple.
3. Cut heart shapes out of red peppers or tomatoes slices.
4. Make some special Valentine cookies.

HEART-PRINT NUT COOKIES

1. Beat together ⅔ cup butter, ⅓ cup sugar, and ¼ teaspoon salt until fluffy.
2. Add 2 egg yolks and 1 teaspoon vanilla. Beat well.
3. Gradually add 1–½ cups flour, beating until well mixed. Cover and chill about 1 hour or till firm enough to handle.
4. Preheat oven to 350°. Shape dough into 1" balls. Roll in a slightly beaten egg white, then in ¾ cup finely chopped walnuts. Place 2" apart on ungreased cookie sheets.
5. Use a small heart-shaped object (perhaps cut out of cardboard, or even a heart-shaped Valentine candy) to press down the center of each ball.
6. Bake for 15–17 minutes or until light brown on bottom. While the cookies are still hot, you may need to press the heart shape into the center again to make the outline more distinct. Cool, then fill the heart-shapes with red jelly.
7. Makes 36 cookies.

HEART-SHAPED SUGAR COOKIES

1. Cream 1 cup margarine and ¾ cup sugar together.

2. Add 1 egg and mix well.

3. Combine dry ingredients: 4 cups flour, 1 teaspoon baking powder, ½ teaspoon soda, ½ teaspoon salt, ¾ teaspoon nutmeg.

4. Add the dry ingredients alternately with ½ cup vanilla yogurt and 1 teaspoon vanilla to the butter mixture and mix well.

5. Shape into a roll; wrap in aluminum foil or plastic wrap and chill several hours or overnight.

6. Preheat oven to 375°.

7. When ready to bake, roll out to ⅛" thickness. Cut with heart-shaped cookie cutter. Bake for 8-10 minutes or until lightly browned on edges. Cool on wire racks. Wrapped dough will store for 1-2 weeks in refrigerator.

ACTIVITIES

VALENTINE PICTURE BOOK

Valentine's Day and love center around the family for a toddler, and making this special personalized book with and for your child will be fun—and special for you both.

■ Plan one page of the book for each member of the family. Each page will be cut from red construction paper, as large as you wish.

■ Gather one picture of each member of the family. Have your child glue one picture on each page of the book. Print the person's name underneath the picture.

■ Cover each page with clear contact paper and trim.

■ Title the book "All My Loves" or "I Love My Family" or "We Are One Big Family of Love" or something similar.

■ Punch a hole at the top left corner of each page and bind them together with a brad or a binder ring.

VALENTINE COLLAGE

Something toddlers love to do and are relatively successful at is gluing. Cut out various heart shapes from different materials—different colored paper, wrapping paper, fabric, whatever else you can think of. Give them to your child along with a large piece of white construction paper and let her glue whatever she wants onto her collage. Let her do as much as she can by herself.

HEART RUBBINGS

Use some of the left-over heart shapes from the collage project and cut some more out of textured materials like cork, sandpaper, wallpaper, canvas, or corrugated cardboard. Let your child make heart rubbings by placing the hearts under sheets of paper and rubbing across the paper with crayons.

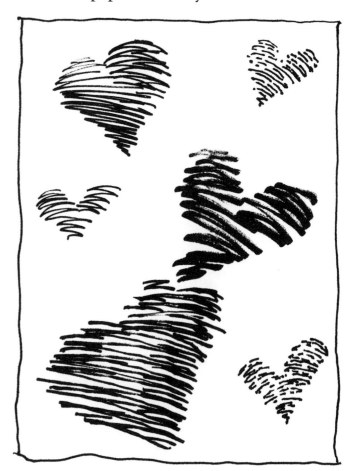

A Week Of Birthdays

Monday's child is fair of face,
Tuesday's child is full of grace,
Wednesday's child is full of woe,
Thursday's child has far to go,
Friday's child is loving and giving,
Saturday's child works hard for its living,
But the child that's born on the Sabbath day
Is bonny and blithe, and good and gay.

Most two and three year olds respond to the word "party" with great excitement and enthusiasm. They don't care whether it's a party for themselves or someone else. They will (help) blow out the candles, open the gifts, and entertain the troops with dancing, singing, and other spunky antics typical of their lively age.

When it's your toddler's birthday, you'll no doubt want to celebrate in style. Telling you to keep your child's age in mind sounds perfectly obvious, but think about it. If she is turning two, for example, she won't care that you invite twenty children to a full afternoon of nonstop entertainment and festivities including everything from Bozo the Clown to Musical Chairs. A few guests invited to share a special birthday snack, a few minutes of play, and a gift exchange is plenty for a two year old. Choose a theme appropriate to your child's interests, like balloons, kitty cats, trucks, dolls, or doggies. Use it for a cake theme, party favors, gifts, and decorating ideas. Do as many simple and appropriate things as you can that will make your child know this is indeed a very special day just for her.

READINGS

Benny Bakes A Cake by Eve Rice (Greenwillow; pb Morrow)

It's Benny's birthday, and since he's a big boy now, Mama asks if he'd like to help bake his cake. They do a wonderful job, but unfortunately, Ralph the dog is the only one who gets to enjoy it! Papa saves the day.

Ask Mr. Bear by Marjorie Flack (Macmillan; pb Macmillan)

It's Danny's mom's birthday, and he wants to give her something very special. He asks all his animal friends if they have any suggestions, and it's not until he asks Mr. Bear that he finds the perfect answer. This is a touching story that's fun for toddlers because of its repetition. It helps a child see the giving side of birthdays.

Max's Birthday by Rosemary Wells (Dial Books for Young Readers)

Max gets a present from his sister, Lucy, and he is not so sure he likes it. By the end of the story, the reader is as convinced as Max that it is a great gift. This board book is fun for toddlers.

There are many other good birthday books—***Happy Birthday, Sam*** by Pat Hutchins (Greenwillow), ***Spot's Birthday*** by Eric Hill (Pitnam), and ***Miffy's Birthday*** by Dick Bruna (Two Continents) are three of them. Look for others as well.

RECITINGS

HAPPY BIRTHDAY TO YOU
(Sung to "Happy Birthday")

Happy birthday to you,
Happy birthday to you,
You look very happy,
And you act like it, too.

Today is your day,
To have things your way.
A cake that's your favorite,
And games you like to play.

(Two) years have passed by,
Time has passed by,
You've added such happiness
Into all our lives.

We hope today will be,
An exciting party.
We love you, dear (Margo),
Thanks for joining our family.

THE BIRTHDAY SONG
(Sung to "The Muffin Man")

Today is someone's special day,
Special day, special day.
Today is someone's special day
It's (Matthew's) Happy Birthday!

Today (Matthew) is three years old
Three years old, three years old.
Today (Matthew) is three years old,
And we love him so.

Let's all wish him a happy day,
Happy day, happy day.
Let's all wish him a happy day,
Filled with love and lots of play.

RECIPES

A SPECIAL BIRTHDAY CAKE

Your child might have a favorite cake, or you might use a cake mix or the recipe that follows. The flavor isn't what really counts—the decorations and the candles do! Choose a theme that will be easy to use on a cake.

■ Balloons, for example: Make a rectangular cake, frost it, and arrange pastel mint wafers in a cluster in the upper corner of the cake, with shoestring licorice for balloon strings. Write "Happy Birthday, (Kate)" on the balloons or on another part of the cake.

■ For a kitty-cat, bake three 8" circle cakes, use one for the head, one for the body, and cut two triangular ears and a crescent tail from the last one.

■ For a train, divide one batch of cake batter among four small loaf pans and bake. Frost them, arrange in a row on a track of licorice and use round mints or lifesavers as wheels. (With little ones, supervise the eating of the candies closely.)

BASIC YELLOW CAKE

1. Preheat oven to 350°.
2. Beat together ⅓ cup margarine and ¾ cup sugar.
3. Add ½ cup milk, 1 egg, and 1-½ teaspoons vanilla. Beat.
4. Add 1-¾ cup flour, 2-½ teaspoons baking powder, and ¼ teaspoon salt.
5. Add ¼ cup more milk. Beat 2 minutes.
6. Pour into greased and floured 8" x 1-½" round baking pan. Bake for 30 minutes.

CHOCOLATE BUTTER FROSTING

1. Beat 3 tablespoons margarine, add 1-⅓ cups sifted powdered sugar.
2. Beat in 1 tablespoon milk, ¾ teaspoon vanilla, and 1 ounce melted unsweetened chocolate.
3. Beat in 1 cup more sifted powdered sugar. Add more milk if you need to make the frosting easier to spread.

LOLLIPOP COOKIES

Cookies on a stick can be a special birthday treat.

1. Preheat oven to 375°.
2. Thoroughly cream together ½ cup margarine and ¼ cup brown sugar.
3. Beat in 1 egg and ¾ teaspoon vanilla.
4. Add ¾ cup wheat germ, ¾ cup flour, ¼ cup semisweet chocolate pieces, ¼ cup flaked coconut, ¼ cup uncooked quick oats, 1 teaspoon baking powder, and ¼ teaspoon salt. Blend well.
5. Roll dough with your hands into 1-½" balls. Place about 2" apart on greased cookie sheets. Insert a wooden stick (such as a clean popsicle stick) half-way into the side of each ball of dough.
6. Dip a flat-bottomed glass in sugar, and use it to flatten the cookies. Decorate cookies if you wish with dried fruit, candies, or nuts.
8. Bake for 12-15 minutes. Makes about 12 cookies.

BIRTHDAY PARTY PLANS

When you plan a party for children, invite only a few children, keep it simple, and limit it to about an hour. Try something like this:

■ Fifteen minutes free play. Set out building blocks, balls, cars, trucks, housekeeping toys, or dress-up things for children to do as they arrive.

■ Fifteen minutes planned activity. One example might be a treasure hunt. Have prizes hidden for everyone—choose three or four different locations and hide enough objects in each location for everyone to find. Use as many clues as the children need.

■ Fifteen minutes eating cake and goodies.

■ Fifteen minutes opening gifts.

BIRTHDAY SIGN

Write "Happy Birthday, Robert," in great big letters on poster board. Spread glue inside each letter and have your child help you sprinkle on glitter, spices, or other decorations to make his birthday sign especially interesting.

BIRTHDAY PIN

Cut out a picture of your child in a circle shape, glue it to some colored poster board or heavy construction paper, write "Happy Birthday to Me" around the picture, cover it with clear contact paper, and attach it to your child's shirt with a paper clip.

BIRTHDAY DECORATIONS

Decorate outdoors by attaching balloons and crepe paper streamers to your mailbox or lamppost; decorate inside with the same items by attaching them to bannisters, dining room chandeliers, or other high places. Have your child help—or do it as a surprise for him.

Little Jumping Joan

Here am I,
Little Jumping Joan,
When nobody's with me,
I'm all alone.

"Me do it myself!" is an almost universal declaration made by two year olds as they struggle to become independent social beings. The desire to step out of babyhood challenges a two year old to try all kinds of new and exciting tasks. Pouring one's own orange juice, climbing the kitchen counters to reach one's own cereal, and dressing oneself all just must be tried. How successful your child is will partly shape her self-esteem. If all her attempts at proving her independence end in frustration, her self-confidence will be greatly diminished. If the tasks are reasonable and your toddler succeeds, she will begin to feel good about her capabilities and about herself as a person.

As parents, we can create situations that will prevent failures and provide successes for our twos and threes. By only partially filling the orange juice container to insure an easy pouring job, by placing acceptable foods on low shelves for them to reach themselves, and by selecting simple clothing (elastic waist, large pull-on tops, velcro shoes) to make dressing easier, we can help our children feel good about themselves.

Take time this week to celebrate your child's uniqueness, her independence, and her "me-ness" as you enjoy some of these activities.

READINGS

How Do I Put It On? by Shigeo Watanabe (Putnam Publishing Group; pb Putnam Publishing Group)

When Bear wants to get dressed all by himself, he discovers it's not as easy as he thought it would be. Although he runs into difficulties, he succeeds, and he feels great because he did it all by himself. This book is the first of an eight-book series of "I Can Do It All By Myself" books. The other seven are equally satisfying to a toddler because Bear always reaches his goals—in his own way—all by himself!

Book 2—***What A Good Lunch***—about eating.

Book 3—***Get Set! Go!***—about overcoming obstacles.

Book 4—***I'm The King Of The Castle***—about playing alone.

Book 5—***I Can Ride It!***—about setting goals.

Book 6—***Where's My Daddy?***—about perseverance .

Book 7—***I Can Build A House!***—about creative play.

Book 8—***I Can Take A Walk!***—about testing limits.

I Can Dress Myself by Dick Bruna (Methuen)

Brother and Sister are proud because they can dress themselves with everything from socks to mittens. Dick Bruna has written many fine books for very young readers. His clear drawings, vivid colors, and simple storyline are perfect for this age. Look for his other titles as well.

I Can—Can You? by Peggy Parish (Greenwillow Books)

There are four board books in this series that suggest various activities for the child to imitate, such as wriggling fingers, brushing teeth, and splashing water.

RECITINGS

LOOK IN THE MIRROR
(Sung to "Frère Jacques")

Look in the mirror, look in the mirror,
What do you see? What do you see?
Two great big blue eyes, two great big blue eyes,
That belong to me, that belong to me.

Look in the mirror, look in the mirror,
What do you see? What do you see?
Curly brown hair, curly brown hair,
That belongs to me, that belongs to me.

Continue by adding more verses appropriate to your child, such as "a face full of freckles," or "a pair of gold-rimmed glasses," or "a tiny little nose."

I AM TWO
(Sung to "Three Blind Mice")

I am two, I am two.
What can I do? What can I do?
I can talk like my Mommy does,
Use my vacuum to pick up fuzz,
Eat with a fork and a spoon because
I am two.

I AM THREE
(Sung to "Three Blind Mice")

I am three, I am three.
Look at me, look at me.
I can climb on my jungle gym,
Put my face in the water to swim,
Share my toys with my cousin, Tim,
Because I am three.

You may wish to add verses more suitable for your own child's accomplishments.

RECIPES

Try these two simple recipes that let your child "do it myself!"

"DO IT MYSELF" CEREAL

1. Have the following ingredients measured out and ready for your child to pour and mix together.

    1 cup quick-cooking oats
    ½ cup wheat germ
    ½ cup diced dried apricots or other dried fruit
    ½ cup chopped walnuts or other nuts
    1 cup shredded wheat or natural (no sugar added) flakes
    ¾ cup raisins

2. Give your child a large bowl. Let her dump all the ingredients in it and stir them up with a wooden spoon.

3. Store in an air-tight jar in the refrigerator for up to 3 weeks. Makes approximately ten servings.

"DO IT MYSELF" JUICE

1. Place one half of a juice orange in a plastic bag. Squeeze most of the air out. Seal the plastic bag.

2. Allow your child to squeeze the orange to get out the juice.

3. Open a corner slightly, insert a straw, and have your child drink her homemade juice.

ACTIVITIES

DO–IT–MYSELF OUTLINE

Take two brown grocery bags, cut them open and tape them to make one long piece of paper; or cut a long piece of brown packaging paper. Have your child lie down on the brown paper. With a magic marker, trace around his body to get his outline. Together fill in his features discussing all the wonderful things that make him "him"!

MIRROR PLAY

Stand in front of a mirror with your child and study your child's face with her. Point out the color of her eyes, the shape of her nose, the details of her lips, the color of her hair, and any other features you feel are noteworthy. Take a piece of soap, and while your child is standing relatively still, trace the image of her head on the mirror. Color in the facial features with the soap and have fun looking at her "double image". There are soap crayons on the market that are perfect for this.

DO–IT–MYSELF ASSIGNMENTS

Think of several things that your child has mastered, such as putting on her shoes, dancing to a particular song, getting an item that you have asked for, "reading" a certain book, and play this game: Take your child's hand and tell her you are going to play a fun game. Lead her to the spot in the house where you'd like to play. Sit down together on the floor. Then give her one assignment at a time to do. Each time she completes an assignment, she can be given a point, a sticker, a kiss, a hug, or whatever you deem appropriate.

FOURTH WEEK

Coffee and Tea

Molly, my sister, and I fell out,
And what do you think it was all about?
She loved coffee and I loved tea,
And that was the reason we couldn't agree.

How many children are in your family? Whether it's one, two, or a dozen, there are advantages and disadvantages to the number.

Psychologists have been fascinated by the effects of place in birth order on personality development. Dr. Lucille Forer, Ph.D., is one of many who have written books exploring this intriguing subject.

Research shows that an only child is often mature and organized, yet may have a tough time sharing. The oldest child in a family has high expectations, knows right from wrong, and in order not to fail at something new, may not try at all. Middle children are durable, independent, and able to make compromises, and they may tend to be procrastinators or make bad compromises. The baby of a family often has the advantage of knowing he can try anything: if he fails, it's all right because he's younger, and if he succeeds, he can beat his older sibling! Twins have a built-in playmate, but they have to work at finding time alone.

Every situation is different, and we need to teach our children to live and be happy with whatever situation is theirs. An older child may not like his pesky younger brother; a young one may feel frustrated that she can't keep up with her older sister. Twins may resent having to share so much of themselves sometimes, and other times, they may love having the bond that only twins can share. We all have to play with the cards we've been dealt. Our job as parents is to try to ease our children into seeing the best of what life has dealt them. The books and activities below will help.

READINGS

A Place For Ben by Jeanne Titherington (Greenwillow)

Ben is feeling crowded out by his baby brother, Ezra, and needs a place of his own. After searching for one, finding it, and getting it ready, he sits down to enjoy it—but finds that something is missing. Only when Ezra comes to visit does Ben realize how he really feels. This is a sensitive and touching story that acknowledges siblings' feelings.

Born Two-gether by Jan Brennan (J&L Books)

With clear language and beautiful photography, this book addresses the various feelings of being a twin. It presents ten different situations and shows a positive as well as a negative side to each situation.

Big Brother by Charlotte Zolotow (Harper & Row)

A big brother is constantly teasing his little sister until one day when his little sister stops reacting. He sees her in a whole different light and things change between them.

If It Weren't For Benjamin (I'd Always Get to Lick the Spoon) by Barbara Shook Hazen (Human Sciences Press)

A younger brother describes his frustrations as well as the advantages of having an older brother. This story is a bit long, but you may wish to share some of it with your child.

RECITINGS

HUSH
(Sung to "Hush Little Baby")

Hush, little (Emily),
Don't you cry,
Your brother really loves you,
And so do I.
Sometimes he may seem nasty and mean,
But it really isn't all that it may seem.
Having to share your life with him,
At times may seem to be so grim.
But think of all the fun you have,
When you play together and feel so glad.
If you search way down in your heart,
You know he's loved you right from the start.
Please remember what I say
When you feel sad like you do today.
Try to tuck your sadness away,
Smile a big smile and enjoy your day.

MY BROTHER, (DAN)
(Sung to "The Muffin Man")

Do you know my brother, (Dan),
My brother, (Dan), my brother, (Dan).
Do you know my brother, (Dan),
He is a friend of mine.

Sometimes we like to fight,
Argue, kick, and scream all night,
But mostly we play so dynamite,
And get along real fine.

RECIPES

HONEY COOKIES
Have your child share them with his "honey" of a friend: his brother or sister.
1. Preheat oven to 350°.
2. Mix together ½ cup margarine, ½ cup peanut butter, ¼ cup sugar, and ¼ cup honey. Beat in 1 egg.
3. Mix in 1-½ cups flour, ¼ teaspoon baking soda, ¼ teaspoon baking powder, and a pinch of salt.
4. Drop by rounded teaspoons about 2" apart onto greased cookie sheets. Bake for about 10 minutes. Cool on cooling rack.

TWIN COOKIES
Twins may look the same on the outside, but they sure can be different on the inside—just like these cookies!
1. Preheat oven to 350°.
2. Mix together ¾ cup margarine, ¼ cup sugar, and ⅛ teaspoon salt. Add 1 egg and 1 teaspoon vanilla.
3. Beat in 1-¾ cups flour. Mix well.
4. Shape the dough into 1" balls. Press one small piece of candy (such as a jelly bean, gum drop, or M&M) into the center of the cookie and shape the dough around it so you can't see the candy. Place the balls about 2" apart on ungreased cookie sheets.
5. Bake for about 15 minutes.
6. Optional: Place ¾ cup sifted powdered sugar in a plastic bag and gently shake the cookies in the sugar to coat lightly.

ACTIVITIES

MY SPOT
Everyone needs to be alone once in a while. Help your child find a little spot in your house to call his own. If he has his own bedroom, it's easy. If not, try being creative

with spaces in your home. There might be a place in the basement, the attic, or a closet. Wherever you choose, let him bring a favorite stuffed animal, a book, a toy, and/or a blanket. Let him set up his spot as he would like.

"YOU'RE OK" TEA PARTY

Have each child draw a placemat picture for one of the other "guests" at the tea party. Have the children dictate a phrase or sentence that they want to tell their brother/sister and you can write the words under the picture. Set the table with the placemats, napkins, "teacups" with tea (juice), and some honey cookies.

COOPERATION GAMES

Arrange some games for your children to play together that will show them how much fun they can have when they cooperate and play well together. Examples might be Treasure Hunts (one child hides a special toy and the other finds it) or Hide and Seek (one hides while the other seeks).

Chapter Three

MARCH

Treasures of Music and Movement

Do you know any two or three year old who can sit perfectly still when there's music playing? I don't! Children respond to music the way popcorn responds to heat. Turn on the music, and every cell in a child's body wakes up and starts dancing. We adults marvel at their energy.

Through the treasures of music and movement, your child not only has a great time and gets a great workout but she also has great learning opportunities. I think you'll both enjoy tuning into the musical fun in this chapter.

Banbury Cross

Ride a cock-horse to Banbury Cross
To see a fine lady upon a white horse;
Rings on her fingers and bells on her toes,
And she shall have music wherever she goes.

"…And she shall have music wherever she goes." We should all have music wherever we go, for a day without music is a poorer day. Some people shy away from it because they aren't accomplished musicians, but you don't have to be a virtuoso to feel the joy of music. And music is just that…feeling. When a musician makes music, he expresses his feelings through the medium of voice or instrument. Drummer, guitarist, and singer are all conveying what they feel inside as they perform their music.

Children are natural musicians, for they have few inhibitions and easily express their feelings. Almost all children love to be part of music, whether by singing, dancing, banging on pots, or tapping a toy xylophone. I encourage you to use this natural enthusiasm and provide as many rich musical experiences and opportunities as you can for your child. You needn't sign your two year old up for formal piano lessons or have him audition for a Broadway musical. What you can do is find entertaining ways to share the feelings of music as you take time out together.

READINGS

Max, the Music-Maker by Miriam B. Stecher (Lothrop, Lee & Shepard Books)

Max finds or makes music everywhere, in the purring of a kitty cat or by banging pot lids. The reader sees how Max experiments with sounds, and the reader is enticed to do the same. This narrative story with black and white photographs captures a boy's musical enthusiasm.

One Light, One Sun by Raffi (Crown)

The sun rises and sets on three families in this picture book song. This book is based on the lyrics of one of Raffi's songs. It is beautifully illustrated.

Three Blind Mice by John W. Ivimey, illustrated by Paul Galdone (Clarion Books)

Inspired by Mother Goose's rhyme, this author wanted to tell what happened before the farmer's wife cut off the mice's tails and then what happened after. Mr. Galdone's illustrations enhance this satisfying tale.

There are several popular performers who have collected favorite children's songs and compiled them into books with piano and guitar music for adults to share with their children. Here are four notable ones.

Lois & Bram Sharon's Mother Goose (pb Atlantic Monthly)

This wonderful illustrated collection of nursery rhymes and songs is for the whole family to share and enjoy. With poems and musical scores, it is both a reading book and a sing-along book.

Hap Palmer Favorites—Songs for Learning Through Music and Movement by Hap Palmer (Alfred Publishing Co.)

The songs are divided into these categories: body awareness, motor skills and self image, socialization, colors, shapes, numbers and letters, rhythms, sing-alongs, and creative movement.

Music for Ones and Twos—Songs and Games for the Very Young Child by Tom Glazer (Doubleday)

A great collection of some of Tom Glazer's songs.

The Raffi Singable Songbook by Raffi (Crown Publishers)

A collection of fifty-one songs from Raffi's first three records for young children.

RECITINGS

SING, SING, SING A SONG
(Sung to "See-Saw, Marjorie Daw")

Sing, sing, sing a song,
First thing in the morning;
What a way to start your day,
To get your spirits soaring.

Sing, sing, sing a song,
While you work and play;
It brings a smile that stays a while,
Makes you feel good all day.

Sing, sing, sing a song,
Before you go to sleep;
A lullaby will pacify,
No need for counting sheep.

THE LEADER OF THE BAND
(Sung to "Farmer in the Dell")

The leader of the band,
The leader of the band,
Heigh-ho, the derry-o,
The leader of the band.

The leader plays a drum, *etc.*
The leader plays a cymbal, *etc.*
The leader plays a flute, *etc.*
The leader plays a trumpet, *etc.*
The leader plays a trombone, *etc.*

Choose others that you and your child know.

You can play a little game if you have a small group of children together. Have the children sit together in the middle of the floor. The leader will march around the other children as everyone sings. As the leader selects the next player, that person joins him and marches along behind him. The other children join the marching band until everyone is playing some "instrument" and marching around the room.

RECIPES

Have a musical snack with your child. As you're making the following recipes with your child, adapt the song "Here we go round the mulberry bush." Sing together, "This is the way we…" filling in what your child is doing to help prepare the food.

MUSICAL MUFFINS

1. Preheat the oven to 400°. and grease a 12-muffin tin. ("This is the way we grease the pans, grease the pans, grease the pans. This is the way we grease the pans, so early in the morning.")

2. Measure 1-¾ cups flour, ¼ cup sugar, 2-½ teaspoons baking powder, and ½ teaspoon salt into a medium bowl. Stir to mix well. ("This is the way we measure the flour …")

3. Beat one egg with a fork, add ¾ cup milk and ⅓ cup oil. Mix well. ("This is the way we beat the egg …")

4. Pour the milk mixture over the flour mixture. Stir with wooden spoon only till the flour is wet. Batter will be lumpy. Do not stir too much, or the muffins will be hard.

5. Spoon half the batter into muffin pans till each cup is about one-third full. Put a teaspoon of jelly or jam on the batter in each cup. Then fill the muffin cup with the remaining batter till it's about two-thirds full.

6. Bake till golden brown, about 20–25 minutes.

MUSICAL MILKSHAKE

Use the same song as you make a shake:

1. Put a 10-ounce package of frozen strawberries (thawed) and their juice into a blender. Cover and blend until smooth. ("This is the way we blend the berries ...")

2. Add 1 cup milk. Blend.

3. Put one large scoop of strawberry ice cream into each of three tall glasses. Put 1 cup of the ice cream into the blender and blend until smooth.

4. Pour mixture into the glasses and serve with a straw and a spoon.

ACTIVITIES

There are countless activities that will involve a child in music. Here are some:

SOUND EXPERIMENTS

■ Matching sounds—Have your child close his eyes while you make pairs of sounds, some the same and some different, to see if he can tell the difference. For example: tap two forks together and tap a glass with a fork for two different sounds. Ask your child if the sounds are the same or different.

■ Fast, slow sounds—Use a metronome, piano, or other instrument to make fast and slow sounds and have your child tell you which each sound is.

■ Loud, soft sounds—Have your child make loud and soft sounds using tennis balls, pot lids, pillows, or wooden blocks.

■ High, low sounds—Partially fill glasses with water and experiment with the difference in sound as more water is added.

■ Long, short sounds—Try blowing on paper to produce a long sound and tapping on paper to produce short sounds.

LISTENING TO MUSIC

Provide music for your child to...
■ Dance to.
■ Move in as many ways as possible to, e.g., crawl, trot, spin, wiggle.
■ March to.
■ Play musical chairs or "Stop" to. (When the music is playing, the child moves or dances, but when the music stops, he does, too.)

MAKING MUSIC

■ Have a variety of toy musical instruments available for your child to experiment with.

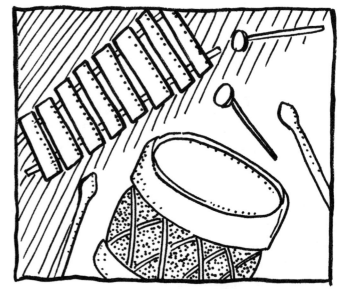

■ Make easy home-made instruments, e.g., "rubberbandjos"—rubber bands stretched over a shoe box.

■ Use your voices as often as you can to sing, sing, sing!

SECOND WEEK

This Is The Way

This is the way the ladies ride,
Trit, trot, trit, trot.
This is the way the gentlemen ride,
Jiggety-jog, jiggety-jog.
This is the way the farmers ride,
Hobblety-hoy, hobblety-hoy.
This is the way the hunters ride,
Gallopy, gallopy, gallopy
Over the fence.

If we could add to this wonderful Mother Goose rhyme, we might say, "This is the way a toddler moves: faster, faster, faster!" Life is full of action for a toddler, and that's why this rhyme is so popular with children. As you recite the rhyme, you bounce your child on your knees. Each verse gets faster and bumpier until the child is galloping and giggling on your knees at the conclusion of the rhyme.

Toddlers don't walk much; they need to run. Toddlers seldom sit long enough to finish a meal; they need to be on the move. Occasionally you might catch a toddler coloring longer than five minutes, but usually she's off again to explore and conquer after making a few quick scribbles. She's always in a hurry: jumping, dancing, climbing, sliding, tumbling, and running. Her very essence seems to center around movement and exploration.

Through all this movement and exploration, a toddler learns about her environment. It's important to allow her as much freedom of movement as possible. Constantly saying "no" to a toddler frustrates and stifles her. Whenever and wherever you can, set up areas that will allow her lots of freedom to move. The activities that follow are some suggestions of ways to support this active and energetic stage in your child's life.

READINGS

Max's Ride by Rosemary Wells (Dial Books for Young Readers)

"'Go!' said Max" are the first words in this book, and that is exactly what Max does. Max is a funny bunny who "goes" nonstop. He delights the reader in each of the eight books in this "Very First Books" series. Each book is small and made of cardboard pages just right for a toddler's hands. The other seven are: **Max's First Word, Max's Toys: A Counting Book, Max's New Suit, Max's Bath, Max's Birthday, Max's Breakfast**, and **Max's Bedtime.**

Freight Train by Donald Crews (Greenwillow; pb Penguin)

This book, a Caldecott Honor Book, shows action through the incredible artwork of Donald Crews. The reader can see the freight train speeding across the pages and thus gets a visual concept of motion. Other action books by Donald Crews are **Carousel** and **Bicycle Race**.

47

Five Little Monkeys Jumping on the Bed by Eileen Christelow (Clarion Books)

This book is based on the favorite nursery rhyme and has an interesting twist at the end.

Touch! Touch! By Riki Levinson (E.P. Dutton)

A toddler can't resist touching everything in sight and sets a whole household in motion.

RECITINGS

WHAT CAN WE DO?
(Sung to "London Bridge")

What can we do when we take time out,
Take time out, take time out?
What can we do when we take time out,
Take time out to play?

Let's play tag when we take time out,
Take time out, take time out.
Let's play tag when we take time out,
Take time out to play!

Let's follow the leader when we take time
    out, *etc.*
Let's play hopscotch when we take time out,
    etc.

Make up more verses about the games you play with your child.

THIS IS THE WAY

This is the way I like to run
All around the house.
This is the way I like to creep
And pretend to be a mouse.

This is the way I like to dance
And sing my favorite songs.
And this is the way I love to hug
Nice and long!

Have your child act out the motions in this poem.

RECIPES

HOPSCOTCH BARS

These delicious bars are named after their light butterscotch flavor—and you can use them as a snack after playing hopscotch with your child!

1. Preheat oven to 350°.
2. Mix 1 cup brown sugar with ¼ cup melted butter.
3. Add 1 egg and 1 teaspoon vanilla. Beat well.
4. Add ¾ cup flour, ¼ cup wheat germ, 1 teaspoon baking powder, and a pinch of salt. Mix well.
5. Add ½ cup chopped walnuts. (Optional: add ¼ cup chocolate chips.)
6. Spread batter in greased 8" x 8" x 2" baking pan. Bake for 20–25 minutes or until edges are firm.
7. Cut into bars while still warm. Makes about 25 bars.

JACK–BE–NIMBLE CANDLESTICK

Another fun snack to eat after an active playtime of jumping—and so easy your child can assemble it herself!

1. Place one pineapple ring on a plate.
2. Stand half a peeled banana up inside the circle of the pineapple.
3. Put a cherry, grape, or other small berry on top of the banana.

48

ACTIVITIES

JACK–BE–NIMBLE JUMPING

Toddlers love to jump, and love to show *you* how they can. Let your child jump distances, or over objects, or down from one step, or wherever else you can think of that's safe. Use this nursery rhyme to play to. You could also provide a pretend candlestick for your child to practice jumping over.

JACK BE NIMBLE
Jack be nimble,
Jack be quick.
Jack jumped over
The candlestick.

MODIFIED HOPSCOTCH

If playing outside, draw a hopscotch grid on the driveway or sidewalk with chalk; if playing inside, use masking tape to mark off the grid.

Make a simplified grid—perhaps four big squares all connected in one even bigger square, or four squares lined up in a row.

Using a beanbag, a flat soft toy, or stuffed animal, have your child toss it into one of the squares. He must then jump into each square and then pick up the beanbag.

FOLLOW THE LEADER

Take turns being the leader and copying each other's actions. Some movements to choose from are jumping up and down, skipping, running, waving arms and/or legs, hopping on one or two feet, and somersaults.

HIKE IN THE HOUSE

Go for a pretend hike in the house. Pack a snack (perhaps the Hopscotch Bars above) and then lead the way. Climb a steep mountainside (the stairs), crawl through a cave (made from pillows and blankets), and invent more interesting landscapes as you go. Give your child a turn at leading, too.

OBSTACLE COURSE

Lay out an obstacle course in your house. Use whatever you have at hand to set up as many different kinds of movement as you can. Crawling over pillows, under chairs and tables, jumping on beds (if you permit that in your house), climbing up stairs, hopping over lines marked on the floor, and running a designated path are all possibilities. Then let your child loose!

THIRD WEEK

Forehead, Eyes, Cheeks, Nose, Mouth, and Chin

Here sits the Lord Mayor,
Here sit his two men,
Here sits the cock,
Here sits the hen,
Here sit the little chickens,
Here they run in.
Chin-chopper, chin-chopper, chin-chopper, chin!

Since the day your child was born you have been "chin-chopping," "pat-a-caking," and "this little piggy-ing" your way into your child's heart. You've been tickling bellies, tweaking noses, and goosing tickle spots. You've been caressing soft cheeks, stroking tired limbs, and massaging relaxed backs. All these tactile experiences are not only pleasant interactive play between parent and child but also expressions of love that deepen your relationship. Through touch, this powerful form of communication, your child feels good as he begins to learn about his own body. You touch *his* nose or tickle *his* belly, and he begins to get a sense of his separate being. He is learning that all of these wonderful things belong to him. At the age of two or three, when a toddler is busy exploring "mine" and "me," he begans showing a sense of pride about *his* body. Tune into this body pride and spend some special moments as you play and talk. (This is also a good time to begin teaching your child personal safety and how to differentiate between good touches and bad touches.)

READINGS

Eyes, Nose, Fingers, Toes by Ruth Krauss (Harper)

This classic is a rhyming bedtime book. After opening with "Eyes, nose, fingers, toes, lips, hair, everywhere," the text goes on to say good-night to each body part.

Here Are My Hands by Bill Martin, Jr. and John Archambault (Henry Holt & Co.)

The simple rhymes and illustrations make this picture book one to be read aloud and acted out.

Tail Toes Eyes Ears Nose by Marilee Robin Burton (Harper & Row, Publishers)

This is a delightful guessing game about eight familiar animals (including man) and their various body parts.

RECITINGS

A GAME TO PLAY
(Sung to "Looby Loo")

Here is a game to play,
Here is a game we like,
We can play it in the day,
We can play it in the night.

We tap our heads like this,
We tap our heads like that,
Tap one and two—once more will do,
So give it one more pat.

Continue with more verses such as:

We tap our tummies, *etc.*
We tap our knees, *etc.*
We tap our toes, *etc.*

WHERE IS?
(Sung to "Where is Thumbkin?")

A: Where is your nose, where is your nose?
C: Here it is, here it is.
A: Touch it with your finger.
C: May I?
A: Yes, you may, sir.
A: Come and play, come and play.

The "A" is for the adult to sing, and the "C" is the child's part. Go on with other body parts you want to include in this little game/song.

Where is your mouth, *etc.*
Where is your neck, *etc.*
Where are your eyes, *etc.*
Where are your ears, *etc.*

RECIPES

BODY TALK SALADS

Give your child a variety of ingredients, and let him make his own "person" salad. Aim for the inclusion of a head, a body, two arms, and two legs—and perhaps the facial features if the face is large enough. Some useful ingredients: cottage cheese, a hard-boiled egg, or a round slice of orange for the head; half a canned or fresh peach or half a canned or fresh pear for the body; carrot sticks, celery sticks, or cheese sticks for arms and legs; and shredded cheese, raisins, nuts, and pimentoes for facial features.

BODY TALK COOKIES

Make this delicious mix-by-hand dough, and then make body shapes—small flat circles for heads, larger flat circles for bodies, four short rolled ropes for arms and legs, and whatever other details you and your child would like to add. Assemble them right on the cookie sheets, then bake.

1. Preheat oven to 350°.

2. Mix 1 cup butter and 1 cup peanut butter with a wooden spoon. Add ¼ cup sugar and ¼ cup packed brown sugar. Stir till mixed.

3. Add 2 eggs and 1 teaspoon vanilla. Stir till mixed.

4. In another bowl, mix 2-¼ cups flour, 2 teaspoons baking soda, and ¼ teaspoon salt. Stir into peanut butter mixture till well mixed. Use your hands to mix if you need to, as the dough is quite stiff.

5. With your hands, shape into balls and ropes. Place them on an ungreased cookie sheet. Flatten and push together the pieces of dough to make the bodies you want. Use little pieces of dough for eyes, nose, etc. Gently press them into the larger pieces of dough.

6. Bake for 10–12 minutes or till light brown on the edges. Let cool on cookie sheet for 1 minute. Makes about 36 cookies.

ACTIVITIES

JIGGLE GIGGLE

Choose rhythmic music to use as a background. Have your child stand facing you, then ask him to jiggle the body part you call out. Call out one by one, "your arm," "your foot," "your head." Allow about ten seconds between each body part so that you and your child can jiggle and giggle sufficiently! Move on to more difficult body parts, such as thigh and calf, to add to your child's body vocabulary.

SEE AND SAY

Use body talk to teach both listening skills and following directions. Give commands such as "touch your fingers to your toes" or "put your hand on your thigh." If he does well and finds this easy, you might want to give two instructions at once, such as "put one hand on your head and the other hand on your waist."

SIMON SAYS

Try a modified, simple version of Simon Says. Give simple commands such as "Simon says, touch your head" while you execute the directions yourself. As you play, remember that with young children the object of the game is not to fool them into doing something that "Simon" didn't "say," but to have fun. Keep the game simple.

CUT-OUT BODY TALK

Cut circles, squares, triangles, and other simple shapes out of construction paper (ahead of time), and then with your child assemble them into a person, talking about parts of the body all the time.

Five Toes

This little pig went to market;
This little pig stayed home;
This little pig had roast beef;
This little pig had none;
And this little pig cried,"Wee,wee,wee!"
All the way home.

The toe touching and tickling associated with this much-loved rhyme are as much a part of the lure as the verse itself. Perhaps a child's fascination with feet begins when, as an infant, she first grabs those wiggling, kicking things that are just within her reach and realizes they're attached to *her*. Whenever it begins, a child's fascination with her feet is a strong one. Toe wiggling, grabbing, and sucking are common pastimes for curious infants. As an infant grows into an active, walking toddler, the fascination continues and is extended to her shoes. A child with brand new shoes is a beaming child. Everyone she sees for at least five days becomes another private audience for showing off her new shoes. Enjoy your toddler's foot fascination as you walk through some of these projects.

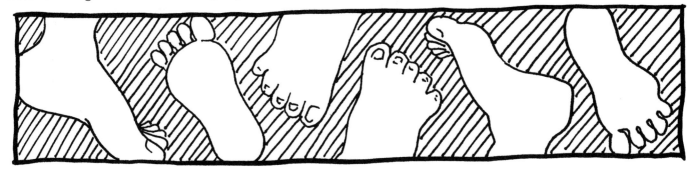

READINGS

The Foot Book by Dr. Seuss (Random)

"Oh, how many feet you meet" in this wonderful rhyming Dr. Seuss book. From fuzzy fur feet to her feet, from sick feet to trick feet—you meet them all. Dr. Seuss acknowledges the young reader's fascination with feet and plays with it in this delightful book.

Alfie's Feet by Shirley Hughes (Lothrop, Lee & Shepard Books; pb Mulberry Books)

Alfie loves to splash in puddles and tramp through mud. When his Mom buys him a new pair of shiny yellow boots, the reader shares his excitement—and his adventures.

Shoes by Elizabeth Winthrop (Harper Junior Books; pb Harper Junior Books)

There are so many kinds of shoes, including those that are too loose, too tight, those to run in and to double flip in. Best of all are the kind we're all born with—our feet! This book shows all of this and more about shoes.

RECITINGS

THERE'S NOTHING LIKE IT

There's nothing quite so neat
As the sound of your feet
In a brand new pair of shoes.
The tapping of new shoes,
The thumping of new boots,
And the squeak-squeaking of sneakers, too.

There's nothing quite so real
As the comfortable feel
Of a brand new pair of shoes.
They hug your toes real tight,
They make you feel just right,
And your feet get so happy and light.

Oh, there's nothing can compare
To the look when you wear
A brand new pair of shoes.
You look but can't believe
That it's you inside of these.
What a great looking pair of feet!

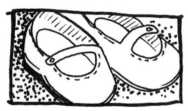

OH, DEAR NEW SHOES
(Sung to "Oh, Suzanna")

Oh, I come from (Soucy's Shoestore)
With new shoes on my feet,
I feel so proud and happy,
And my feet now look so neat.

My old shoes were all worn out,
All the way down to their soles.
My toes were squashed and crowded
And were peeking out the holes.

Oh, dear new shoes,
You look so good to me.
I am so glad that we bought you,
I'll take care of you, you'll see.

RECIPES

Prepare this funny, "punny" breakfast and start the day off in celebration of feet!

FRENCH TOES-T

1. Beat 2 eggs till foamy. Add ½ cup milk and ½ teaspoon vanilla. Beat till well mixed. Pour into a pie plate.

2. Dip a slice of bread into the egg mixture, then turn it over to soak the other side. Put the bread in a warmed-up skillet with 1 teaspoon butter melted in it.

3. Cook till underside of bread is golden brown. Flip and cook other side.

4. Repeat steps 2 and 3 until all the egg mixture is gone. You'll probably use four pieces of bread.

5. Serve as is or cut into the shape of a foot.

FrOOT SALAD

No, you don't mix this salad up with your feet. You make the salad in the shape of feet!

1. Take one fresh pear and cut it in half the long way. Scrape out seeds and stem. Put half the pear on a plate, cut side down. (Or use canned pear halves)

2. Use one of the following or something similar to make five toes at the wider end of the pear: peanuts, mandarin oranges, small berries like blueberries or raspberries, small strawberries, or pineapple tidbits.

ACTIVITIES

HOKEY POKEY

Do some "happy feet" dancing to your favorite music, or teach your child the "Hokey Pokey" and enjoy doing that together.

You put your right foot in,
You put your right foot out,
You put your right foot in,
And you shake it all about.
You do the Hokey Pokey
And you turn yourself around.
That's what it's all about!

Face each other as you sing the song and do what the song suggests. Continue the song with the left foot, right arm, left arm, head, whole self, or any other body part you choose.

FOOTPRINTS

Make footprints by one of the following two methods.

■ Spread fingerpaint on paper, stick your child's bare foot in the paint, then have her step onto a new sheet of paper to make a print. Do it again until you have as many footprints as you both want. Let the footprints dry, and then cut them out.

■ Trace your child's foot onto a piece of colored construction paper, and then cut it out. Trace her foot as many times as you want footprints (which can be fun), or simply use the first as a pattern and copy it. Watch out, many feet are ticklish when lightly touched with the side of a pencil!

Use these footprints in the following game.

FIND ME

Have one person be the hider and the other be the seeker. The hider takes the footprints and makes a trail for the seeker to follow to help find where she has gone.

MATCHING SHOE GAME

Take out several pairs of shoes belonging to different members of your family. Mix them up and ask your child to match them and line them up in pairs.

Chapter Four

APRIL

Springtime Treasures

There are so many spring treasures. One glance outside reveals delicate buds of leaves and flowers; one sniff of the gentle breeze treats you to fragrant aromas of new life budding; one step outside lets you feel the sun's strengthening warmth. There are signs of spring everywhere— from daffodils to rainstorms, from Easter bunnies to longer daylight hours. Share them all with your little one as you treasure these beautiful days together.

Daffodils

Daffy-down-dilly has come to town
In a yellow petticoat and a green gown.

To an adult, spring is a time to rejoice in the beauty of crocus and daffodil, to welcome the robins' return, to bask in the sun's golden warmth and enjoy longer days. To a child, spring is a time to play outside on the swingset, play outside in the sandbox, play outside on tricycles and hotwheels, and play, play, play outside! A toddler and the outdoors go together like a honeybee and a field of spring flowers. Plan your days around the weather and do as many outdoor things as you can. Welcome these glorious days with your child as you do some of the springtime activities.

READINGS

Honey Rabbit by Margo Hopkins (Western Publishing)

When Honey Rabbit asks his daddy what spring is, his daddy tells him to go look around the meadow to see for himself. When Honey Rabbit does, he encounters friends who each help him to see another special part of spring. This is a tender look at spring through an animal's eyes.

It's Spring, Peterkin by Emilie Boon (Random House)

Peterkin and his two animal friends observe several spring treats as they spend a beautiful spring day outside. The simple illustrations and board pages make this a good spring book for toddlers.

Hamilton Duck's Springtime Story by Arthur Getz (Golden Press)

Hamilton duck goes out for a walk on a beautiful spring day to see all the treasures of spring. He gets a big surprise that delights us all.

Spring by Colin McNaughton (Dial Books for Young Readers)

This board book is part of a series of four, one for each season. Simple drawings and one-word explanations show children involved in activities typical of the season.

RECITINGS

HERE WE GO ON A SPRINGTIME WALK
(Sung to "The Mulberry Bush")

Here we go on a springtime walk,
A springtime walk, a springtime walk.
Here we go on a springtime walk,
So early in the morning.

Let's look for some signs of spring,
Some signs of spring, some signs of spring.
Let's look for some signs of spring,
So early in the morning.

I can see some pussywillows,
Some pussywillows, some pussywillows.
I can see some pussywillows,
So early in the morning.

Add more verses as you find things on your walk.

I can see some red-breasted robins, *etc.*
I can see some robins' eggs, *etc.*
I can see some daffodils, *etc.*
I can see some flowers growing, *etc.*

A SPRINGTIME WISH

I know there are four seasons,
Spring, summer, winter, and fall.
But I have many reasons
Why spring's the best of all.

I love to hear the birds sing
In the morning when I wake.
Chirps and tweets and trillings
Are some of the sounds they make.

I love to see new plants grow,
The flowers are so bright.
My garden food's so good, you know,
We eat it day and night.

The birds and plants are only two
Of the wonderful things of spring.
I wish warm, springlike days for you,
And all the joy they bring.

RECIPES

Flowers are a beautiful source of spring excitement, so here are some "flower" recipes to add to the springy mood.

FLOWER SALADS

1. Use various vegetable combinations to make flower designs. For example, place a carrot slice in the center of a plate, with celery slices fanning out around it in a starlike fashion, and then cut a stem and leaf from a green pepper.

2. Use various fruit combinations to make flower designs. For example, place a banana slice in the middle with other banana slices or orange segments fanning out around it in starlike fashion; or cut grapes in half, arrange them in a circle, and put a strawberry in the middle.

3. You may wish to offer a variety of cut-up fruits and vegetables to your child and let him make his own flowers.

FLOWER PIZZAS

1. Preheat oven to 425°.

2. For a crust, use either toasted English muffins, 1 package refrigerator biscuits, or your own pizza dough recipe.

3. Spoon about 1-½ tablespoons pizza sauce onto each crust. Sprinkle each crust with 1-½ tablespoons of shredded mozzarella cheese.

4. Let your child top her own flower pizza. Use sliced pepperoni, chopped green pepper, sliced olives, sliced mushrooms, or other toppings she likes.

5. Bake about 10 minutes.

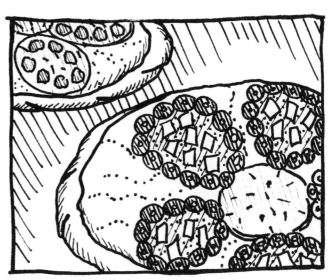

FLOWER COOKIES

1. In a large mixing bowl, beat 1 cup butter and ½ cup sugar till fluffy.

2. Add 2 tablespoons milk and 1 teaspoon vanilla.

3. Gradually beat in 2-½ cups flour till well mixed. Divide into 4 parts. Wrap each part in clear plastic wrap and chill in refrigerator for 2 hours or till firm enough to roll out.

4. When ready to roll, preheat oven to 375°. Take one section of dough out of the refrigerator at a time, roll on a lightly floured surface to ¼ inch thickness.

5. Here is the fun part. Use a flower-shaped cookie cutter and then decorate. Use chopped nuts, chocolate bits, Cheerios, cornflakes, or small cinnamon candies. Put decorations in muffin tins so they'll be handy. Use a garlic press to squeeze some dough into spaghetti-like pieces for stems. Mix cocoa powder with water to draw brown lines with a toothpick. Use cotton swabs to paint with a mixture of water and food coloring. You may have other ideas for decorations.

6. Repeat with remaining dough.

7. Bake for about 8 minutes or till the edges are light brown. Makes 36–48 cookies.

ACTIVITIES

SPRING WALK

This must be the most obvious and yet the best thing to do! Take a walk with your child and observe as many spring things as you can. Look for pussywillows, berries, leaf buds; for flowers, like crocuses, daffodils, and tulips; for robins and baby animals. You may wish to take the same walk each week to see the changes that take place so rapidly during the spring. You may also wish to give your child a pail or bag in which to collect various spring items of interest. Make sure he doesn't pick growing, living things. Explain why to him.

SPRING NATURE BOX

When you return from your walk, have your child put her collected nature things into an egg carton. If she has up to six things, put each one in a section and then label the section above it; if there are up to twelve things, label right in the same section. Remove the lid, and cover the filled egg carton with clear contact paper to save its contents.

PUSSYWILLOW PICTURES

Use cottonballs, glue, brown crayon, and construction paper to make these easy and fluffy spring pictures. Draw a branch on a large piece of construction paper with the brown crayon, and then have your child glue on cotton balls to complete the pussywillow picture.

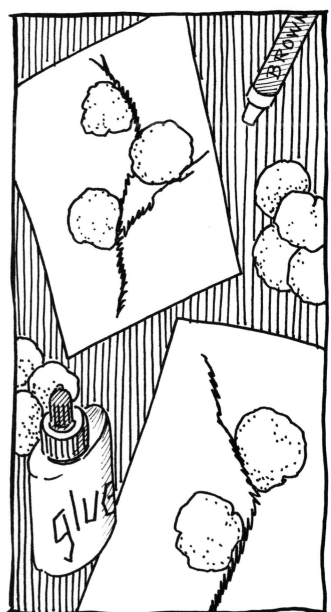

SECOND WEEK

Rain

Rain, rain, go away,
Come again another day;
Little children want to play.

Who says children can't play when it's raining? Certainly not the children. They don't see rain as a deterrent to play—they see it as a new medium with which to experiment. Rain makes puddles where there was once only dry pavement. Rain makes mud where there was once only dry dirt. From a child's point of view, puddles and mud are two *wonderful* results of rain. And, of course, there are always delightful things to do inside for which there never seems quite enough time. Take advantage of rainy days by enjoying some of the offerings below.

READINGS

Rain by Robert Kalan, illustrated by Donald Crews (Greenwillow)

This simple concept book is a mesmerizing visual story of a rainstorm. It shows the progression from blue sky and yellow sun to white and gray clouds, on to the rainstorm, and finally to a beautiful rainbow.

My Red Umbrella by Robert Bright (Morrow Junior Books; pb Morrow Junior Books)

A little girl finds her red umbrella to be a shelter for many animal friends during her brief walk in the rain. The young reader will love to see the umbrella gradually grow as it accommodates more and more animals.

Rain Rain Rivers by Uri Shulevitz (Farrar, Straus & Giroux; pb Farrar, Straus & Giroux)

This beautiful look at rain includes such exquisite phrases as "I'll jump over pieces of sky in the gutter."

Listen to the Rain by Bill Martin, Jr. and John Archambault (Henry Holt & Co.)

This is a great read-aloud book with lovely words and soft pictures for a rainy day.

RECITINGS

WHEN THE RAIN COMES POURING DOWN
(Sung to "When the Saints Go Marchin' In")

Oh, when the rain
Comes pouring down,
Oh, when the rain comes pouring down,
I want to be outside playing,
When the rain comes pouring down.

And when the rain
Makes lots of puddles,
Oh, when the rain makes lots of puddles,
I want to be outside playing,
When the rain makes lots of puddles.

And when the rain
Makes drippy leaves,
And when the rain makes drippy leaves,
I want to be outside playing,
When the rain makes drippy leaves.

And when the rain
Makes flowers grow,
And when the rain makes flowers grow,
I want to be outside playing,
When the rain makes flowers grow.

RAIN
(Sung to "Rain, Rain")

Rain, rain,
Came so fast,
One blink ago it was sunny.
This storm raced in, drenched us and then
Blew away—how funny!

RECIPES

RAINY-DAY TEA PARTY

Home-baked bread is two treats: first its delicious fragrance, and then the tasty bread itself. It isn't all that much work involved, but it'll take about 3 hours. Plan accordingly!

CINNAMON-OATMEAL BREAD

1. Melt ⅓ cup margarine and ½ cup honey in 1-½ cups of water in a saucepan on the stove. Cool for 10 minutes.

2. In a large mixing bowl, stir together 5 cups white flour, 1 cup quick oats, 2 tablespoons dry yeast, and 1 teaspoon salt.

3. Add the cooled liquid. When mixed in, add 2 eggs, and mix.

4. Knead dough for 5 minutes, adding 1-½ to 2 cups more flour as needed.

5. Spread 1 tablespoon oil in a clean large mixing bowl. Form dough into a ball and put it in the bowl, turning the dough ball so the top gets oiled, too. Cover the bowl with a towel, put it in a warm place, and let it rise about 1 hour or until it doubles in bulk.

6. Punch dough down. Divide into 2 balls.

7. Grease two 8" x 4" loaf pans with 1 tablespoon butter.

8. Mix together 4 tablespoons butter, ¼ cup sugar, and 2 teaspoons cinnamon.

9. Flatten each dough ball into thin rectangles as wide as the loaf pans are long. Spread the butter mixture on the surface of each dough rectangle, and then sprinkle on ¼ cup raisins. (Raisins are optional.)

10. Starting at the shorter edge, roll each rectangle as tightly as you can. Place each in a buttered pan with the seam side down. Cover with towel and let rise again for 30 minutes.

11. Preheat oven to 350°.

12. Spread 1 tablespoon butter over the tops of loaves. Bake for 35 minutes.

FRUIT TEA

A great accompaniment to the cinnamon bread. To 6 cups water, add 1 tea bag, 1 cinnamon stick, 1 whole clove, 1 orange cut in wedges, and 1 lemon cut in wedges. Let the mixture steep for 3 minutes. Stir well, then serve with extra orange and/or lemon sections.

ACTIVITIES

OUTDOOR RAIN FUN

With the proper clothes, a rainy day can be wonderful for your toddler. With boots, slicker, and umbrella, he's almost impervious to the rain. Puddle-splashing and mud-squishing are fine for a short play period outside. (Perhaps you can go while your bread is baking, and then come inside to warm, dry clothes, a house fragrant with baking bread, and delicious tea party treats!)

INDOOR RAIN FUN

■ Rain Cuttings—Give your child a pair of safety scissors and let him cut little pieces of white construction paper or aluminum foil. Any shape will do. He can glue these shapes onto black or blue construction paper as his raindrops. Cutting is fascinating for a toddler once he masters some control of the scissors. Give him the freedom to make whatever kind of rainstorm he wants—one with tiny drops or one that is raining "cats and dogs." You might want to try using a paper punch to get different raindrop shapes, too.

■ "Rain" Shower—Why not enjoy a "rain" shower inside? Take an umbrella into the shower and turn the water on! Let your child listen to the sounds the "rain" makes. It could end there, or you might turn it into a drenching downpour in which the umbrella gets blown away. You can let this activity go as far as you wish it to.

THIRD WEEK

One to Ten

1, 2, 3, 4, 5,
I caught a hare alive.
6, 7, 8, 9, 10,
I let it go again.

Have you ever tried to catch a hare? Or better yet, have you ever seen the Easter Hare? Yes, the Easter Hare, as Egyptian mythology says! The tradition of the Easter bunny reaches back to ancient times, when the hare was an animal sacred to the goddess of spring, Eastre. When the hare laid its eggs in the garden, it symbolized the return of spring—a renewal of life.

Easter traditions all center on a theme of renewal. In the Christian world, Easter is a renewal of life as celebrated in the resurrection of Jesus. In the natural world, Easter is a renewal of plant and animal life as celebrated in the coming of spring. And in a child's world, Easter is a renewal of excitement as celebrated with the annual visit from the Easter bunny.

Encourage Easter anticipation as you enjoy some of these bunny activities.

READINGS

Bunnies are one of a toddler's favorite animals, and there are many books that feature them. Some are specifically about Easter while others are just about bunnies. Several are suggested below.

I Am A Bunny by Ole Rison, illustrated by Richard Scarry (Western Publishing Co.: Golden Books)

One of Richard Scarry's earliest books, this one takes a bunny named Nicholas through the seasons of the year, showing the changes that take place outdoors.

Little Bunny Follows His Nose (a Golden Scratch and Sniff book) by Katharine Howard (Western Publishers)

In this book, your child shares Little Bunny's adventure as he finds various fragrant things to smell.

The Runaway Bunny by Margaret Wise Brown (Harper & Row Junior Books; pb Harper & Row Junior Books)

When a little bunny wants to run away, his mother assures him that she will run after him because he is her little bunny and she loves him. This is a tender and very reassuring book for parents to share with their little ones.

Where Is It? by Tana Hoban (Macmillan) and ***Where's the Bunny?*** by Ruth Carroll (Walck) are two cute bunny books. ***The Golden Bunny*** and ***The Golden Egg Book*** by Margaret Wise Brown (both Golden Press) are two books specifically about Easter suggested for children aged three to six.

Meet Peter Rabbit by Beatrix Potter (Warne)

Every child should get to know the wonderful stories of Beatrix Potter, and now even the youngest of children can be introduced to them. ***Meet Peter Rabbit*** is one of a series of eight board books that introduce toddlers to the Beatrix Potter world. The pictures are the same as in the originals but the text is greatly abbreviated. Peter's sisters, Flop-

sy, Mopsy, and Cottontail, go picking black-berries down the lane, but Peter goes to Mr. MacGregor's garden, where he runs into trouble.

If your child seems ready for the whole original story, pick up **The Tale of Peter Rabbit** by Beatrix Potter (Warne) for a start, then go on to the many other stories in the series.

RECITINGS

I'M A LITTLE BUNNY
(Sung to "I'm a Little Teapot")

I'm a little bunny,
Soft and sweet,
Here are my ears and here are my feet.
When I'm in the garden, I look for treats,
And nibble on all I like to eat.

MY BUNNY HOPS ALL THROUGH THE GARDEN
(Sung to "My Bonnie Lies Over the Ocean")

My bunny hops all through the garden,
My bunny hops all through the yard;
I like to play tag with my bunny,
But trying to catch him is hard.

Come back, come back,
Oh, come back, my bunny to me, to me;
Come back, come back,
Oh, come back my bunny to me.

My bunny is so soft and spunky,
My bunny is a friend to me;
My bunny is such fun to play with,
Come join us and you, too, will see.

RECIPES

BUNNY SALAD
To make two bunny salads:

1. Tear 4 lettuce leaves in shreds and make lettuce nests on two small plates.

2. Place half a pear, cut side down, in each nest.

3. Have your child create her own bunny. Use thin apple wedges for ears, raisins or whole cloves for eyes, a cherry or strawberry for the nose, a pile of coconut for the tail.

BUNNY BREAD
Makes 4 bunnies.

1. Mix 3 cups flour, 2 packages of yeast, and 3 tablespoons salt in a large bowl.

2. Heat 1 cup water, 2/3 cup milk, and 3 tablespoons butter to 125° to 130°. Stir into yeast mixture.

3. Stir in 1 egg. Stir in 2–3 cups more flour to make dough easy to handle. Turn onto lightly floured surface and knead until smooth and elastic. Cover and let rest 10 minutes.

4. Lightly grease 2 cookie sheets. Divide dough into 4 equal parts.

5. For each bunny, use one part. Divide that one part in half. Shape one half into a flattened round for the body, and place on cookie sheet. Take the other half and divide it in two. Use one piece for the bunny head; flatten it and place it next to the body.Use the other piece to make two ears and two feet. Place ears next to head. Make deep indentations in body for feet; press feet into body and flatten.

7. Repeat to make the other three bunnies.

8. Cover and let rise slightly for 15–30 minutes.

9. Bake in 400° oven until light brown, about 18–20 minutes. Decorate as desired.

ACTIVITIES

THIS LITTLE BUNNY
Use the following activities with this bunny poem:

THIS LITTLE BUNNY

This little bunny has two big eyes,
This little bunny is oh so wise.
This little bunny is white as milk,
This little bunny is soft as silk.
This little bunny nibbles away
At cabbages and carrots every day!

■ Cut from construction paper five little bunnies and several cabbages and carrots. As you recite the poem to your child, have her move the appropriate shapes on a table to make a little show.

■ Have your child use her fingers to show the five little bunnies as you recite the poem.

■ Draw five little bunnies on paper for your child. Give her five cottonballs and glue, and have her glue on the cottontails as you recite the poem.

EGGSHELL BUNNY

Draw a bunny on construction paper and cut it out. Give your child colored eggshell pieces saved from Easter eggs. Have her place the eggshells on the bunny in any way she wants. Then take clear contact paper and apply it over the eggshells. Cut out the bunny shape, and you have a colorful, decorated Easter bunny.

CIRCLE BUNNY

Take 1-½"-wide strips of construction paper. Overlap and glue the ends into circles. Use one for the body of the bunny, a smaller one for the head, two tiny ones for the feet. Pinch a crease into each of two more circles to make them into elongated ears. Staple or glue the pieces together, punch a hole in the top to attach a piece of yarn or string, and hang it in a window or doorway. Have your child do as much of this art project as he can.

FOURTH WEEK

Wee Willie Winkie

Wee Willie Winkie runs through the town,
Upstairs and downstairs in his nightgown;
Rapping at the window, crying through the lock,
"Are the children all in bed?
For now it's eight o'clock."

To assure a peaceful bedtime, two conditions must be met: first, enough time must be allowed for carrying out the usual bedtime routine, and second, the appropriate setting must be established, one that is quiet, calming, and dark. When these two things have been taken care of, a child is more easily convinced to climb into bed. You can control all the conditions except one: darkness. Daylight Savings Time takes our bedtime darkness away, leaving a room full of light to contend with! How do we convince a toddler it's time for bed when there aren't even any stars in the sky to make a wish on? It may take an extra measure of patience and/or ingenuity, and at the end of the day, those may not come easily. But don't despair. With the help of these suggestions, you can do it!

READINGS

Goodnight Moon by Margaret Wise Brown (Harper & Row Junior Books; pb Harper & Row Junior Books)

This classic bedtime book, written in 1947, is still loved by everyone who reads it. It follows a bunny through his bedtime ritual of saying goodnight to everything in his bedroom.

Grandfather Twilight by Barbara Berger (Putnam Publishing Group)

Every night, Grandfather Twilight performs a very special task. The reader gets to share in this evening magic as Grandfather Twilight goes for his nightly walk. The incredible illustrations complement the simple and poetic text perfectly.

Where Does Brown Bear Go? by Nicki Weiss (Greenwillow Books)

When it's bedtime, where do the animals go? This question is answered in this warm bedtime book.

Several other fine bedtime books for toddlers include: **Goodnight Owl** by Pat Hutchins (Macmillan), and **Goodnight, Goodnight** by Eve Rice (Morrow). **The Baby's Bedtime Book** by Kay Chorao (Dutton) is a wonderful collection of bedtime poetry to read with your little one.

RECITINGS

SLEEP, SLEEP
(Sung to "Rain, Rain")

Sleep, sleep,
Time for sleep,
Day is done, time to count sheep.
A kiss and hug for you to keep,
I wish you magic dreams, my sweet.

TEN MORE MINUTES
(Sung to "Ten Little Indians")

One little, two little, three little minutes,
Four little, five little, six little minutes,
Seven little, eight little, nine little minutes,
Ten more minutes, please.

Ten more minutes to finish my book,
My castle isn't done yet, take a look,
We never ate the muffins that we cooked,
I'm just not ready, you see.

What's that you say? Tomorrow's another
    day,
With much more time and games to play,
I am kind of tired—well...O.K.,
I guess I can agree.

Ten little, nine little, eight little minutes,
Seven little, six little, five little minutes,
Four little, three little, two little minutes,
One...and it's bed for me.

Some other favorite Mother Goose bedtime rhymes:

The man in the moon
Looked out of the moon
And this is what he said,
"'Tis time that, now
I'm getting up,
All babies went to bed."

Diddle, diddle, dumpling, my son John,
Went to bed with his trousers on,
One shoe off, and one shoe on,
Diddle, diddle, dumpling, my son John.

Star light, star bright,
The first star I see tonight,
I wish I may, I wish I might,
Have the wish I wish tonight.

RECIPES

Have your child help you make these treats to leave out on the kitchen table for a before-breakfast snack.

CHEERIO NECKLACE
Cut a piece of heavy string long enough to make a long necklace for your child's neck. Give him Cheerios to thread onto the string. When he has enough Cheerios on, tie the ends together and let him wear it. When hunger strikes, he can nibble on his necklace!

CEREAL SAMPLER
Make a mixture of cereals (including wholesome cereals like Shredded Wheat, granola, and Cheerios) and dried fruit (like raisins, apricots, and pineapple). Put a small amount in a paper cup, cover with plastic wrap, and leave out on the table for a next-morning snack.

ACTIVITIES

Bedtime routines are extremely important to toddlers. Once they are established, they need to be followed faithfully to assure a pleasant bedtime for your little one.

BEDTIME ROUTINE
If you don't already have a set routine, plan one. Some general considerations might include a time to pick up toys; a bath, brushing teeth, and other cleaning routines; a reading time; a final drink of water; hugs and kisses.

BEDTIME POSTER

Once you have your routine established, make a poster or a book to refer to that shows all the parts of the bedtime routine. Keep it simple. For a poster, divide the oaktag into sections in which you will draw simple illustrations of the bedtime things that must be done each night. For example, draw several simple toys for clean-up, a toothbrush for personal clean-up, a book for reading time, a cup for last drink, and lips for kisses. If you choose to make a book, use the same kind of illustrations and bind the book together with tape or staples. If you'd like, you can print single words under each picture to help identify them for your child.

BEDTIME DRINK

READING TIME

CLEAN-UP

BRUSHING TEETH

GOODNIGHT KISS

MORNING TREAT

Sometimes bedtime is easier if the child has something to look forward to the next morning. Choose something simple to leave out on the kitchen table for your child to do in the morning when he gets up. The snacks above are two possibilities, but the treat doesn't have to be food. It could be a coloring book and crayons, a favorite stuffed animal, a book to look at, or a favorite toy. Let him put the chosen object on the table just before going to bed so he will feel more in control of his bedtime.

Chapter Five

MAY

Treasures of the Great Outdoors

Good weather brings more outdoor treasures, and during the month of May, there are so many to be found. Everything is out there waiting to be discovered and enjoyed—butterflies and frogs, playgrounds and gardens.

Take some of the books suggested in this chapter and go outside. Find a cozy spot and read them to your little one. Plan to spend time enjoying the great outdoors together.

See-Saw

See-saw, Margery Daw,
Jacky shall have a new master;
Jacky must have a penny a day,
Because he can't work any faster.

Clean fresh air, a crystal blue sky, and the warm golden glow of the sun entice us outdoors. Even more inviting to a toddler are seesaws, swings, slides, monkey bars, trees, tricycles, sandboxes, and balls. For most children, playing outdoors beats playing indoors, hands down. Perhaps it's because of the freedom a child feels as he runs like the wind, the freedom of being outside four constraining walls. Every game takes on a new dimension when played in the wide open space of outdoors.

With the weather improving by the day and colors blossoming almost by the hour, you can take advantage of this fine outdoor playground. You don't need special equipment; you don't need to go to a playground or park. Just head outside with your child, and you'll find plenty of opportunities to play.

READINGS

Lily Goes to the Playground by Jill Krementz (Random House)

Lily spends some time at the playground. We see her running, sliding, climbing, seesawing, pretending, riding, building a sandcastle, and having great fun in this enjoyable board book for toddlers.

The Playground by Kate Duke (E.P. Dutton)

This board book shows mother and child guinea pigs spending a day at the playground. We see all the familiar favorite activities.

When We Went to the Park by Shirley Hughes (Lothrop, Lee & Shepard Books)

Grandpa and his granddaughter see lots of special things on their visit to the park. They count up all the treats they see, and the reader can count along.

RECITINGS

SWINGING, SWINGING
(Sung to "Sailing, Sailing")

Swinging, swinging,
Stretching for the sky,
How I love to swing and glide,
I feel like I can fly!

Swinging, swinging,
I feel so big and tall,
Swinging is an outdoor treat,
My favorite thing of all!

WHAT SHALL WE DO WHEN WE GO OUT?
(Sung to "The Mulberry Bush")

What shall we do when we go out,
We go out, we go out.
What shall we do when we go out,
When we go out to play?

We will ride our three-wheel bikes,
Three-wheel bikes, three-wheel bikes.

We will ride our three-wheel bikes
When we go out to play.

We will see-saw up and down,
Up and down, up and down.
We will see-saw up and down
When we go out to play.

Add other verses if you'd like.

RECIPES

MONKEY BARS

These are so named because there are bananas in them, not because they look like playground equipment.

1. Preheat oven to 350° and grease a 15" x 10" x 1" baking pan.

2. Beat ¾ cup butter till softened. Add ⅓ cup sugar and ⅓ cup brown sugar. Beat till fluffy.

3. Beat in 1 egg and 1 teaspoon vanilla.

4. Stir in 1 cup mashed banana (about 3 medium bananas).

5. Gradually add 2 cups flour, ¼ cup wheat germ, 2 teaspoons baking powder, and ¼ teaspoon salt. Beat till well-mixed.

6. Add ½ cup semi-sweet chocolate pieces, ¼ cup chopped walnuts, and ¼ cup shredded coconut.

7. Spread batter in greased pan. Bake for 25 minutes.

SUNRISE JUICE

1. Fill juice glass ⅔ full with apricot nectar. Tilt glass and slowly add cranberry juice. Notice the lovely sunrise—now it's time to go out to play!

ACTIVITIES

Any activity played outdoors on a beautiful day is generally a hit. Take some of your child's favorite games outside. The games will change out there, with more running and exercise involved. For example, you can play Simon Says, Follow the Leader, Hide and Seek, or Tag with slightly different rules than you use indoors, and have a wonderful time. Here are some other ideas:

BALL TOSS GAME

Bring out several laundry baskets and several large balls. Set up fair distances, then have your child try to make "baskets" by throwing the balls into the baskets.

BALL–KICKING PRACTICE

Stand opposite your child and kick a ball back and forth to each other. As your skills improve, widen the space between you to make the task harder.

BUBBLE BLOWING

Blowing bubbles is always great fun, whether you use the store-bought jars of bubbles, or make your own by combining equal quantities of water and liquid dishwashing soap.

TRIKE PATH

Make up a path for your child to ride her trike. If you have a driveway, draw with chalk a particular "road" on which she can ride. If she will be driving on grass, mark the road off with objects like rocks or outdoor toys. Use whatever you have available.

WATER PLAY

Fill a kiddie swimming pool, a large dishpan, or an old baby's bathtub with water. Let your child play with water toys. Toy boats, paper cups, funnels, plastic containers, measuring cups, and the like would be appropriate.

SAND PLAY

Take out all the sand toys and let your child sand-castle to his heart's delight.

SECOND WEEK

Miss Muffet

Little Miss Muffet
Sat on a tuffet,
Eating her curds and whey.
Along came a great spider
And sat down beside her,
And frightened Miss Muffet away.

Why do spiders and other insects frighten us? Is it the general appearance of particular bugs that intimidates? Surely there are more pleasant things to look at than spiders! Are we afraid they'll hurt us? If you've ever been stung by a bee, you can agree with that! Do the ways they have of annoying us give them their bad reputation? That's true for flies, certainly.

In spite of our shudders at spiders and other bugs, there are positive and important reasons for these creatures to exist. Spiders catch and eat other harmful insects. Without bees, there would be no honey. And even the pesky fly has some merit in the eye-hand coordination gained through fly swatting!

This is the time of the year when all these interesting bugs will be surfacing again. Spend some time teaching your child about them: what they look like, where they live, what they do, what they eat, and if they will bother people or not. The activities below will help you focus your spring attention on bugs, bugs, and more bugs.

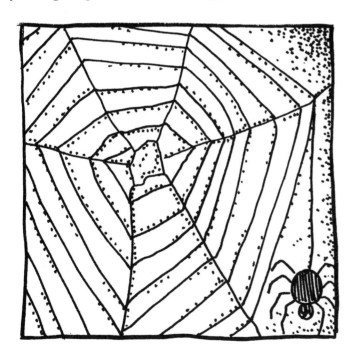

READINGS

The Very Busy Spider by Eric Carle (Putnam Publishing Group; pb Putnam Publishing Group)

This clever hands-on book follows the development of a spider web as a little spider weaves a web right in it. The reader traces the growth of the web, which starts with a thin raised line and progresses to a full-page tactile maze as the busy spider readies the web to catch a fly.

Buzz Buzz Buzz by Byron Barton (Macmillan)

When a bee stings a bull, it sets off a chain reaction that comically comes right back around to where it began.

The Bear and the Fly by Paula Winter (Crown)

This funny wordless picture book shows Daddy Bear trying to swat a pesky fly that interrupts him and his family during dinner.

RECITINGS

THE EENSY WEENSY SPIDER AND THE BROWN AND YELLOW HONEYBEE

The eensy weensy spider went up the water
    spout.
Down came the rain and washed the spider
    out.
Out came the sun and dried up all the rain,
And the eensy weensy spider went up the
    spout again.

The brown and yellow honeybee flies flower
    to flower,
Gathering sweet nectar hour after hour.
He brings it all back like a good little bee,
Where he makes some yummy honey for
    you and me.

WHEN THE BUGS COME OUT IN SPRING
(Sung to "When the Saints Go Marching In")

When the bugs come out in spring,
Oh, when the bugs come out in spring,
I want to be outside watching,
When the bugs come out in Spring.

I'll see some crawl, I'll see some fly,
I'll see so many passing by.
I'll watch and see how many I know,
Of the bugs that come in spring.

I'll see some ants and wasps and bees,
Butterflies and moths I'll see,
Flies and spiders and mosquitoes,
When the bugs come out in spring.

RECIPES

LITTLE MISS MUFFET'S CURDS AND WHEY

What are curds and whey anyway?! Curds are the solids left when milk curdles, and whey is the liquid. You can explain Little Miss Muffet's snack by actually making some with your child.

1. Warm 1 cup whole milk and add ½ teaspoon vinegar or lemon juice. Stir as curds form.

2. Strain the curds from the whey. Blot the curds on a paper towel and gently press them with more towels to get out the liquid.

3. Sprinkle with a tiny bit of salt, and refrigerate.

4. Eat as a cottage cheese or with flavorings like cinnamon or vanilla. Spread on crackers. Curds mixed with peanut butter is good, too.

BEEHIVE MUFFINS

1. Preheat oven to 375°.

2. Put paper liners in 18 muffin cups.

3. Beat together 1 stick margarine and 1 cup sugar until light and creamy.

4. Add 4 eggs one at a time, beating after each addition.

5. Add 1 cup flour, 1 tablespoon cornstarch, 1 tablespoon baking powder, and ¼ teaspoon nutmeg. Mix well.

6. Add ½ cup milk and mix till blended.

7. Add 1-½ cups more flour, then ½ cup more of milk. Mix

8. Add ½ cup mini-chocolate chips.

9. Spoon into muffin cups and bake 20 minutes.

10. While muffins are cooling, make frosting below.

LEMONY FROSTING

1. Combine 1 cup confectioners' sugar, 1 stick margarine, and ⅓ cup cream cheese, mix until smooth and creamy.

2. Add 1 teaspoon lemon juice. Beat. Add 1 tablespoon milk and 1 drop yellow food coloring (if desired). Blend for 30 seconds.

3. Using a table knife, spread the frosting in hive-shaped, swirled mounds on the cupcakes and sprinkle chocolate jimmies over the frosting.

ACTIVITIES

BUG IDENTIFICATION

Draw or cut from magazines pictures of various bugs—spiders, bees, flies, mosquitoes, ants, whatever you find. Take the pictures outside with you and your child and go on a "treasure hunt" to see if you can find creatures that match your pictures.

BUG SQUARE

Find a sandy, muddy or moist part of the yard where you can section off a square either by drawing it in the dirt with a stick or marking it off with sticks laid along its edges. Take a magnifying glass and study the ground in this section for several minutes to see what's alive in there. You will be amazed at how much you can see. If the spot you have chosen isn't very busy, move to another location. You might also like to do this with spider webs. Find one and observe it closely with a magnifying glass.

FEELY BUGS

Cut a large bug shape out of oaktag. Have your child cut various materials and glue them to the bug to make it a true feely bug. Have available such things as yarn, felt, cotton, carpet samples, and discarded fur.

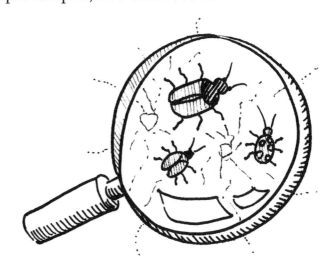

Butterflies

Baby bye, butterfly
Let us watch him, you and I;
There he goes, on his toes,
Tickling baby's nose, nose, nose.

Butterflies are intriguing. Their rich colors make them a popular pattern used in countless designs. Their beauty and presence all around us make them the most sought-after insect among amateur collectors. But an even more amazing feature about the butterfly is that its life changes so dramatically, beginning as a fuzzy crawling caterpillar and ending as a fragile flying creature! A child delights in everything about this insect, from the thrill of the soft tickling touch of the caterpillar to the challenge of trying to net that elusive flying butterfly. Springtime gives us the chance to observe caterpillars and butterflies. Have some caterpillar/butterfly fun with your little one.

READINGS

The Very Hungry Caterpillar by Eric Carle (Putnam Publishing Group; pb Putnam Publishing Group)

This thoroughly enjoyable story of a tiny caterpillar's metamorphosis into a beautiful butterfly is also a manipulative book with holes for young fingers to probe. The book teaches the days of the week, the numbers from one to five, and things about various kinds of food. It is simply and cleverly illustrated, and children love it.

Squiggly Wiggly's Surprise by Arnold Shapiro (Price Stern Sloan)

Another clever story about a caterpillar's metamorphosis, this one teaches colors and has an attached finger puppet for the child to manipulate while enjoying the story.

Hi, Butterfly! by Taro Gomi (Morrow)

A cute peekaboo book where a little boy tries to catch a butterfly in his net but keeps getting tricked.

RECITINGS

BUTTERFLY
(Sung to "Brahm's Lullaby")

Butterfly, what a sight,
In the sky you are lovely,
Flitting here and dancing there,
Making rainbows in the air.

You are quick, you are light,
You are graceful and bright,
You amaze all who see,
As you dance from tree to tree.

SHE'LL BE CHANGING TO A BUTTERFLY REAL SOON
(Sung to "She'll Be Coming Round the Mountain")

She'll be changing to a butterfly real soon,
She'll be changing to a butterfly real soon,
She'll be changing to a butter, she'll be
    changing to a butter,
She'll be changing to a butterfly real soon.

She's a brown and furry caterpillar now, *etc.*
She crawls here and there and everywhere
    today, *etc.*
Someday soon she'll spin her own home—a
    cocoon, *etc.*
Several weeks will pass with no movement at
    all, *etc.*
Then one day she'll come out—a lovely but-
    terfly, *etc.*
No more crawling on the ground, she's air-
    borne now, *etc.*
What a miracle—the life of a butterfly! *etc.*

RECIPES

CATERPILLAR/BUTTERFLY LUNCH
Make all of the following and have a special lunch with your child.

BUTTERFLY SANDWICH
Make a sandwich of your choice and cut
the sandwich on the diagonal to make two
triangular pieces. Put them on a plate, slightly
separated with the pointed sides facing
towards each other. Peel and clean a whole
small carrot but do not cut off the pointed end.
Slide that (pointed end down) between the two
sandwich halves. Use tiny pieces of raisins to
put "eyes" on the carrot-face and make antennae out of carrot curls, sprouts, or thin celery
slices.

CATERPILLAR SALAD
Clean a stalk of celery and cut it in half
crosswise. Fill it with cream cheese. Stick either
sunflower seeds or carrot slices into the cream
cheese. Put raisins sticking out from under the
celery as feet, and use a radish or a nut for a
head.

BUTTERFLY SALAD
Cut four round slices of carrot or apple and
put them on a plate two above two others as
the wings. Put a small stalk of celery in the
middle of the four rounds for a body. Use tiny
pieces of raisins for eyes and thin curly threads
of celery as antennae.

CATERPILLAR DESSERT
Cut three grapes in half, line them up in a
straight line on a plate, put raisin feet and
raisin eyes in the appropriate places, and there
you have it!

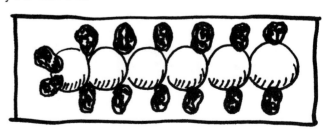

ACTIVITIES

THUMBPRINT CATERPILLARS AND BUTTERFLIES

Using paint, ink, or any other medium you are comfortable with, let your child make thumbprints. For a caterpillar, have your child press three thumbprints right next to each other in a straight line, then use a pencil, magic marker, or crayon to draw in eyes and feet. For a butterfly, press two thumbprints next to each other for the wings, then draw in the rest of the butterfly's body. Experiment and make other interesting designs and backgrounds.

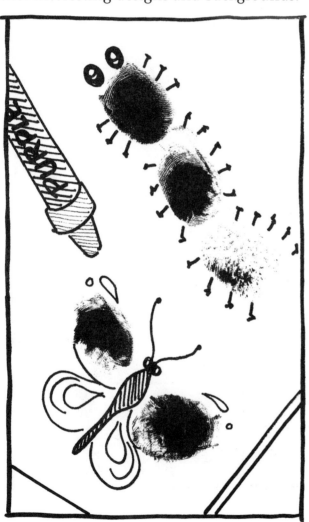

PAPERCHAIN CATERPILLARS

Cut strips 8" x 2" out of colored paper. Make a loop out of the first one by either gluing or stapling the ends together. Loop the next piece of paper through the first, and fasten it with glue or a staple. Continue in this fashion until your "caterpillar" is as long as you and your child want it to be. Glue round black eyes to one end and black little feet along the body if you wish.

BUTTERFLY THEATRICS

■ Act out the life cycle of a butterfly—egg, caterpillar, cocoon, butterfly—with your child. Have him scrunch up into a ball on the ground (egg stage), then begin crawling around like a caterpillar, then find himself a nice little spot to wrap up in a blanket (his cocoon), later to emerge a beautiful flying butterfly (using the blanket as the wings). You may need to perform this first to show your child.

■ Pretend your child is a butterfly by making antennae out of pipecleaners fastened to a headband, and by donning a colorful blanket spread across the back and held onto in each hand. Let your child flap around the house, flying as much as she'd like.

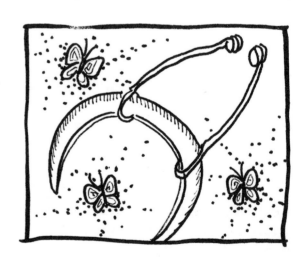

FOURTH WEEK

Gardening

Mary, Mary, quite contrary,
How does your garden grow?
With silver bells and cockle shells,
And pretty maids all in a row.

If you think gardening isn't for a toddler, just put a spade in her hand and watch her go! If you think a toddler can't care for a growing garden, just put a watering can in his hand and watch him go! Of course, if you are a Victory Garden graduate and unsatisfied with anything less productive or esthetic than showplace gardens, you'll need to make certain compromises. Gardening is rewarding and fulfilling for anyone who participates in its miracles of growth, even for a toddler. To see a tiny seed grow into an edible vegetable or a beautiful, colorful flower is awesome. The rewards of a little toil in the soil are plentiful and fun for young and old alike. Take some time to plan your planting time with your child. The activities and suggestions below will help you.

READINGS

The Carrot Seed by Ruth Krauss (Harper Junior Books; pb Harper Junior Books)

This is a beautiful story about an innocent child's faith in a carrot seed he plants. Even when everyone else gives up hope, he believes—and he's there to see the "fruit" of his patience.

Teddy Bear Gardener by Phoebe and Joan Worthington (pb Puffin Books)

Teddy Bear works hard in his garden and enjoys his bountiful crops of flowers and vegetables. This is one in a series of books about Teddy Bear. Others include ***Teddy Bear Baker***, ***Teddy Bear Coalman***, ***Teddy Bear Farmer***, and ***Teddy Bear Postman***.

Peterkin's Very Own Garden by Emilie Boon (Random House)

Peterkin plants his very first garden and encounters both the joys and frustrations of gardening. He solves the problems very well. This is a Great Big Board Book for toddlers.

RECITINGS

A-PLANTING WE WILL GO
(Sung to "A-Hunting We Will Go")

A-planting we will go,
A-planting we will go.
We'll plant some seeds,
Give them what they need,
And then we'll watch them grow!

GO ROUND AND ROUND THE GARDEN
(Sung to "Go Round and Round the Village")

Go round and round the garden,
Go round and round the garden,
Go round and round the garden,
To see what we have grown.

We see some ripe tomatoes,
We see some ripe tomatoes,
We see some ripe tomatoes,
Tomatoes that we've grown.

We see some green bell peppers, *etc.*
We see some tender green beans, *etc.*
We see some long cucumbers, *etc.*
We see some leafy lettuce, *etc.*
We see some crunchy carrots, *etc.*
We see some skinny zucchini, *etc.*

RECIPES

INDOOR GARDENING FRUIT SALAD
1. Take the fruit of 1 orange, 1 grapefruit, and 1 pineapple and dice them up. (See first activity below for further explanation of what to do with the seeds from these fruits.)
2. Add other fruit you like, such as bananas, grapes, apples, pears, strawberries, or blueberries.

3. Cut a 2" slice off the top of a cantaloupe and a ½" slice off the bottom (bottom slice is to give the melon a flat base to sit on). Scrape out the seeds. Use a melon-baller to scoop out balls of cantaloupe to add to your fruit salad.

4. Use the melon shell as the container in which you serve the salad. If you'd like, make a racing car out of the "serving bowl" by cutting four "wheels" out of the 2" section you cut off the top and securing them in place with toothpicks so that they look like wheels.

GARDEN SALAD
WITH CHUNKY HERB DIP
Use a rectangular plate or serving tray and arrange vegetables in rows, as in a garden. Make, for example, a row of cherry tomatoes, a row of green beans, a row of peas, a row of cucumber slices, and a row of carrot rounds.

Serve it with the following dip:
1. Place 1 tomato, 1 scallion cut into small pieces, and ½ a red or green pepper in a food processor and process until the vegetables are small chunks.
2. Add ½ cup plain yogurt, ½ cup cottage cheese, ½ teaspoon chopped fresh basil, and a pinch of salt. Process until well blended.

ACTIVITIES

INDOOR GARDENING
Indoor gardening is fun any time. There are several different things you and your child can do.

■ Take the seeds from an orange, grapefruit, or lemon and plant them ½ inch deep in potting soil. It will take several weeks for the seeds to sprout. (You may wish to soak them in water for a day before planting to give them a head start.)

■ Cut off the top of a pineapple and trim off 3 rows of bottom leaves. Let it dry for 3 days. Then plant it 1" deep in soil. Keep it moist and sunny.

■ Take an onion that's already sprouted and plant it in soil.

■ Suspend the large end of an avocado seed in a jar of water, using 3 toothpicks pushed in on the sides. Sprout in partial sunlight. When a stem is about 4–5" tall, plant it in soil.

■ Cut off the top of a carrot and trim off all the leaves. Place it in a layer of pebbles in a flat dish. Keep it well watered.

MORE INDOOR GARDENING

■ Give your child some large seeds, such as bean or pea seeds, and have him plant them in styrofoam cups filled with soil. When the sprouts seem strong enough and the outdoor soil is ready, he can transplant the plants outdoors.

■ She can also watch a seed sprout by putting it in a plastic baggie with a wet paper towel, keeping it in the sunlight, and watching what happens in several days.

■ You might also want to sprout sprouts! They are among of the easiest and fastest plants to watch grow. You can purchase seeds for sprouting in health food stores or some grocery stores.

OUTDOOR GARDENING

If you can, have a separate little garden patch for your child to call his very own. Show him how to get the soil ready by tilling, show him how to plant the seeds in rows, and then show him how to care for the plants by watering and weeding when the time comes. Let him do as much of the gardening as he wants in his own patch. Some suggested seeds that are large enough for little hands to handle: corn, beans, peas; zinnias, marigolds, calendula, aster and morning glory.

GARDENING ART

Have your child make her garden artistically. Either give her pictures cut from catalogs, seed packages, or magazines which he can glue into a collage, or have her draw the plants in her garden. You can help draw, if you both wish.

FIFTH WEEK

Frogs

Five green and speckled frogs sat on a speckled log,
Eating some most delicious bugs, yum, yum.
One fell into the pool where it was nice and cool.
Then there were four green speckled frogs, blub, blub.

What creature buries itself in mud at the coming of fall and remains inactive until the first warmth of spring? What creature lays about forty-five hundred eggs each year, though only a few survive to develop into adults? What creature peels off its skin and eats it when it gets too tight? None other than the frog.

Frogs are full of changes and surprises. From egg to tadpole to full grown adult, a frog experiences transformations which offer exciting experiences for children to watch and learn. Enjoy this fascinating creature with your child as you explore some of the activities below.

READINGS

A Boy, a Dog, and a Frog by Mercer Mayer (Dial Books for Young Readers)

This is the first of a series of books about the adventures of these three characters. All the wordless picture books in the series tell the amusing stories as well as words ever could! The others titles are: ***Frog, Where Are You?***, ***Frog Goes to Dinner***, ***Frog on His Own***, and ***A Boy, a Dog, a Frog, and a Friend***.

Jump, Frog, Jump by Robert Kalan (Greenwillow)

As a frog jumps his way through his day, the reader gets an idea of what a frog's life is all about.

Seven Froggies Went to School by Kate Duke (E.P. Dutton)

This is a fun-filled rhyming story about seven active and adventuresome frogs who frolic their way through life.

RECITINGS

FIVE SPECKLED FROGS *(continued)*

Four green and speckled frogs sat on a
   speckled log,
Eating some most delicious bugs, yum, yum.
One fell into the pool where it was nice and
   cool,
Then there were three green speckled frogs,
   blub, blub!

Continue on with the poem, changing the number as the frogs fall into the pool.

MARY HAD A LITTLE FROG

Mary had a little frog,
Little frog, little frog,
Mary had a little frog,
Its skin was green as grass.

And everywhere that Mary went,
Mary went, Mary went,
Everywhere that Mary went,
The frog would jump and splash!

I'M A LITTLE TADPOLE
(Sung to "I'm a Little Teapot")

I'm a little tadpole,
Small and frail,
Here is my head and here is my tail.
When I get all grown up,
A frog I'll be,
So watch me grow, it's fun, you'll see.

RECIPES

FROG SALAD

1. Cut ¼ of cucumber, leave the skin on, and stand it on a bed of lettuce.

2. Slice two thin pieces of a green olive and secure them with toothpicks for the frog's eyes.

3. Cut a thin smile line out of the cucumber for the frog's mouth.

4. At the base of the frog, make his four legs by using either celery pieces or pickle spears cut to the appropriate sizes.

LILY PAD SALAD

Make this salad and have your child pretend to be the frog eating the tasty "bugs" offered on the lily pad.

1. Place a lettuce leaf on a plate.

2. Place raisins, golden raisins, nuts, seeds and other dried fruits on the lettuce.

3. Scoop them up with your "sticky" tongue and enjoy your "buggy" treat!

ACTIVITIES

FROG PUPPET

The late Jim Henson has probably done more for the image of the frog than anyone through his wonderful muppet character, Kermit the Frog. Most children know Kermit and love him. If you already own a Kermit puppet, take him out and have your child play with him. If you don't, make one!

Begin with an old green sock. Put your hand in the sock and position your fingers to make a face for the puppet—your thumb is the chin and your four fingers on top are the head. Sew large round button eyes on the head. If you want your frog to have arms and legs, use green felt to cut them out (webbed feet and all) and sew them on where they look the most natural. This is very basic and simple; be more elaborate if you wish, but this will suffice!

FROG MUSIC

On a warm spring evening go to a pond with your child and listen for some frog music. You'll be amazed at the sounds you will hear. Listen for the "jug-o-rum" of the bullfrog, the "tchung" of the green frog, the trill of the common frog, the peep of the peeper frog, the "grunt" of the meadow frog and the "burp" of the pickerel frog. Bring a flashlight along to try to see some of the frogs hopping into the water as you approach.

TADPOLE WATCH

Catch some frogs' eggs to watch the transformation into tadpoles right in your own prepared jar. Take a gallon jar and put about 1" of sand in it. Add a few stones and water plants. Pour in some pond water, with a little scum, until the jar is about ¾ full. Take a few frogs' eggs and put them in the jar. (You should be able to find some in a pond. They look like clear little jelly-balls with black centers. They're usually stuck together in clumps.) Your child (and you) will be fascinated!

LEAP FROG

Certainly don't overlook the old favorite game of Leap Frog. If your child doesn't know this wonderful game already, teach him now. You'll have to scrunch down as tightly as you can for your child to be able to leap over you, but it will be fun!

Chapter Six

JUNE

Summertime Treasures

The gorgeous weather of the summer draws us all to the out-of-doors. It is nearly impossible to stay inside on those glorious early-summer days. There is much awaiting you and your toddler outside. Animals of all kinds, domestic and wild, are fun to observe. New flowers bloom, gardens are in, and as a special treat, strawberries ripen this month. Enjoy the treasures afforded you and your toddler by this pleasant summer season.

FIRST WEEK

Pets

I love little Pussy,
Her coat is so warm,
And if I don't hurt her,
She'll do me no harm.

So I'll sit by the fire,
And give her some food,
And Pussy will love me
Because I am good.

Kids and pets are a natural combination. Just picture a little boy cuddling his fluffy kitten or a little girl caressing her floppy-earred puppy, and you'll see pure contentment and unconditional love. Pets can add an enriching dimension of love to our lives. It's very important for a child to learn to share some of her love for her parents with others, and pets are good practice. Loving and caring for a pet helps children develop a sense of being partially responsible for and in unity with all living things.

Today's life styles, however, often make it difficult for families to keep certain pets. With both parents working and with busier schedules, it sometimes seems unfair (to dogs and cats especially) to raise pets in homes that are often empty for much of the day. But even if your household doesn't include pets, you can still offer your child varied animal experiences. Neighbor's pets, petting zoos, animal shelters, and class pets are some ways to expose your child to animals. The activities offered below can be enjoyed by families with and without pets of their own.

READINGS

Just Like Archie by Niki Daly (Penguin USA)

When Tom finds a snail in the garden, he rushes into the house to make a home for his new-found pet. But "Archie" is not as excited about being Tom's pet as Tom is about having him, and Tom learns a subtle but important lesson about pet ownership.

Emma's Pet by David McPhail (Dutton; pb Dutton)

Emma wants a big, soft cuddly pet and sets off to find one. Her search takes her to all kinds of animals that aren't big, soft, or cuddly, but she does eventually find exactly what she is looking for.

At Mary Bloom's by Aliki (Greenwillow; pb Penguin)

Mary Bloom's house is one filled not only with love but also with animals, and this delightful story shows the ultimate pet owner.

Our Puppy's Vacation by Ruth Brown (E.P.Dutton)

It is Puppy's first vacation, and he's thrilled with everything new and exciting he sees. The reader will frolic through this wonderful adventure along with this energetic puppy.

Good Dog, Carl by Alexandra Day (Green Tiger Press)

This beautifully illustrated wordless book shows how a Rottweiler named Carl cares for the baby while his master and mistress go out. Carl gets into a good bit of mischief, but the adults are none the wiser when they get home.

RECITINGS

There are many Mother Goose rhymes about animals. Include some of your favorites such as "Old Mother Hubbard," "Mary Had a Little Lamb," and "Little Bo-Peep."

MY KITTEN

I have a little kitten,
Her name is Calico,
I pet her and take care of her,
Because I love her so.

Add other verses by changing the name of the kitten and see if you can come up with other ending rhymes.

I have a little kitten,
Her name is Little One.
I pet her and take care of her
Because she is such fun.

"KIWI"
(Sung to "Bingo")

There was a boy who had a cat,
And (Kiwi) was her name, O!
K-I-W-I, K-I-W-I, K-I-W-I,
And (Kiwi) was her name, O!

Substitute whatever is appropriate for your family. You may need to change the boy to a girl, the cat to a turtle, Kiwi to Pokey—whatever! This song will work no matter what you fill in.

RECIPES

FRIENDLY DOG SALAD

1. Take a canned pear half and place it upside down on a bed of lettuce with the neck pointing to the right. (The neck becomes the dog's nose.)

2. Decorate this dog face by using a raisin for the eye, a prune for the ear, a cherry for the nose and two mandarin oranges as a collar (or any other substitutions you and your child like).

KITTY CAT SANDWICH

1. Make one and one-half sandwiches of your choice.

2. Cut the whole sandwich into a large circle, using a knife to round off the edges; cut two small triangular ears from the half sandwich.

3. Place the round sandwich on a paper plate (as the kitty's head), then add the two triangles for ears at the top of the head.

4. Decorate the kitty's face by using two cherry tomato halves for the eyes (or cucumber rounds, or olives, or any other round vegetable), one raisin for the nose, six 1½" to 2" pieces of cooked spaghetti for the whiskers, and one small tomato wedge for the mouth.

Serve goldfish crackers with this "Pet Lunch" to finish off the meal.

ACTIVITIES

ANIMAL GAMES

There are lots of animal games you may like to play with your child. Some of them require more than two people, so you can either adapt the game to fit your own situation or add a few neighborhood children!

■ Cat and Mice Game—One child is the cat and hides. The rest of the players are mice and sneak up to the cat's hiding place and scratch. This is the signal for the cat to chase the mice and try to catch one.

■ Dog and Bone Game—One child is the dog and sits on a chair at a distance in front of the other players. The dog closes her eyes and has her back to the others. The dog's "bone" (choose something to represent the bone) is placed behind the dog's chair. One of the other players tries to sneak up to touch the bone without the dog hearing her. If the dog hears her, she turns around and says, "Bow-Wow." The game begins again with another player trying to sneak up on the bone.

■ Poor Kitty—One child is chosen to be the kitty. The rest of the players sit in a circle on the floor. The kitty crawls on all fours and sadly stops by each person to say "meow." That person must pat the kitty's head and say, "Nice kitty," without even the trace of a smile. The first person to smile, laugh, or giggle becomes the new kitty.

ANIMAL PUPPETS

There are so many different kinds of puppets that you can make with your child—and so many different kinds of animals to make! Choose your child's favorite animal first, then

determine which kind of puppet would be most appropriate. Choose from sock puppets, paper bag puppets, stick puppets, felt puppets, or any others you have the time and talent to do.

PET VISITS

If you know someone who has a pet and is willing to talk about it and share it for a few minutes with you, plan a little visit to that person's home. It could be a common kind of pet that this owner happens to love very much or it could be something unusual like a tame chipmunk or a talking mynah bird. Let your child ask questions, and then let the owner tell whatever she'd like about her pet. This is a great way to expand your child's interest and knowledge about pets from firsthand experiences.

PET COMMANDS

Little ones love to boss around family pets. If your pets know and obey commands, teach your toddler to give the commands and praise the pet when the pet complies. A toddler can feel very grown-up and capable if she can get the dog to sit or shake or come.

SECOND WEEK

The Little Bird

Once I saw a little bird
Come hop, hop, hop;
So I cried, "Little bird,
Will you stop, stop, stop?"

And was going to the window
To say, "How do you do?"
But he shook his little tail,
And far away he flew.

Birds interest many of us, young and old, and for good reason. They are often beautiful to look at, pleasant to hear, and intriguing to study. Their colors span the rainbow from the vibrant red cardinal to the sunny yellow grosbeak to the brilliant indigo bunting. Their calls can bring us hours of melodic tranquility, and their lives make good subjects for study.

Of particular interest to children, especially at this time of year, is the hatching of baby birds. If you can find a nest with eggs in it, it only takes about three weeks for those eggs to hatch, and what an exciting thing it is for your child to observe! From egg to wet, cold hatchlings to fluffy, down-covered chicks to strong flying adults is fascinating development to watch.

Whether you find a nest with eggs this spring or just see the flurry of busy springtime activity among birds, enjoy these special creatures with your child.

READINGS

A Year of Birds by Ashley Wolff (Putnam Publishing Group; pb Penguin)

Ellie is an observant little girl who takes notice of the many birds who visit her house. Each month of the year brings different birds, and each page of this book brings different treasures to cherish. A warm, and rich book that all ages will love.

The Baby Cardinal by Ellen Galinsky (Putnam)

Black and white photographs accompany the text of this story about the early life of a baby cardinal and what he encounters one day when he falls out of his nest.

Benedict Finds a Home by Chris Demarest (Lothrop, Lee & Shepard Books)

Life is too crowded and noisy in the nest for Benedict, so he goes off to find a place of his own. The pictures are comical and the ending is perfect.

RECITINGS

BIRD'S EYE VIEW
(Sung to "He's Got The Whole World In His Hands")

He sees the whole world while he flies.
He sees the whole wide world while he flies.
He sees the whole world while he flies.
He sees the whole world while he flies.

He sees the grasses and the trees while he flies.
He sees the butterflies and bees while he flies.
He sees the oceans and the seas while he flies.
He sees the whole world while he flies.

He sees the people walking while he flies.
He sees the children talking while he flies.
He sees the animals stalking while he flies.
He sees the whole world while he flies.

He sees the cities and towns while he flies.
He sees the buildings all around while he flies.
He sees the cars drive up and down while he flies.
He sees the whole world while he flies.

BIRD IN FLIGHT
(Sung to "Over the River and Through the Woods")

Over the river and through the woods,
The mommy bird flies so free;
She's looking for food,
To serve to her brood,
Of babies, one, two, three.

Over the river and through the woods,
In search of worms and seeds;
No time to play on this busy day,
With so many mouths to feed.

RECIPES

YUMMY EGG NESTS
Make this breakfast recipe to start your Bird-Awareness Day!

1. Preheat oven to 350°.
2. Separate the white from the yolk of an egg. Beat the white until stiff enough to form peaks.
3. Heap the stiff white onto a hot, buttered English muffin. (You may wish to add a slice of American cheese and/or a thin slice of ham on top of the muffin.) Make a hole in the center of the mound.
4. Slip the egg yolk into the hole.
5. Bake until the meringue whites are browned and the yolk is as you like it.

BIRD NEST COOKIES
1. Beat together ½ cup margarine and one 3-ounce package of cream cheese till softened and well-blended. Add ¼ cup sugar and ¼ teaspoon almond extract.
2. Add 1 cup flour, 2 teaspoons baking powder, and a pinch of salt. Beat till well mixed.
3. Cover and chill the dough for 1–2 hours.
4. While it's chilling, prepare the "grass" for the nest. In a screwtop jar, combine 1 teaspoon water, 3 drops of green food coloring, and 1-⅓ cups of coconut. Cover and shake till all the coconut is tinted.
5. Heat oven to 350°.

6. Remove dough from the refrigerator. Shape the dough with your hands into 1" balls. Roll each ball of dough in the tinted coconut till thoroughly coated. Place them 2" apart on ungreased cookie sheets.

7. Bake for 12–15 minutes or till edges are firm. While cookies are still hot, press a jelly bean or nut in the center of the cookie. Makes about 40 cookies.

8. If you'd prefer not to use food coloring, try crumbling Shredded Wheat and use that as the outer coating.

ACTIVITIES

BIRDS' NESTS

Go for a walk with paper bags in hand and collect things a bird might use to make a nest, such as twigs, leaves, pieces of string.

After the walk, have your child fold down the sides of the bag to form the "nest." Then set the bag outside so birds can really use the contents for nest building.

CIRCLE BIRDS

Ahead of time, cut a 4½" circle and a 2½" circle from any color construction paper. Have your child glue the large circle (the body) and the small circle (the head) onto a large piece of paper. Use felt-tip markers to decorate the bird with legs, beak, and feathers as he wishes.

OR, cut out 3 large circles and 1 small circle. Staple the small circle and one large one together to form the body and head. Then fold the other two large circles in half and glue them on as wings. Decorate and use string to hang this bird from window, door, or ceiling.

FEATHER PAINTING

Experiment with using feathers as paint brushes. See what different patterns and lines they can make.

BABY BIRDS IN NESTS

Have your child glue one small cotton ball to the inside of one cup cut from an egg carton. Decorate this "baby bird" with a triangular beak cut from orange construction paper and two plastic moving eyes.

BIRD CALLING AND OBSERVING

Perhaps the most exciting activity of all is to go outdoors and look for some birds to observe. Find a place where you've seen birds before and where you won't be noticed easily, and then settle in with your child. Try this easy bird-call to see if you can attract any birds near you: repeat "pssh...pssh...pssh" in a rhythmic pattern, varying the pattern according to your liking. The birds will respond quickly, if they're going to at all.

THIRD WEEK

The Farmer in the Dell

The farmer in the dell,
The farmer in the dell,
Heigh-ho the derry-o,
The farmer in the dell.

If you wonder why children are so fascinated with farms, take a child and go to one. It probably isn't the lush plants and vegetables that attract the children, or even the big farm equipment working in the fields. You're likely to find your child (and yourself) absorbed in the world of the farm animals. Where else might you pet a soft lamb, feed baby bunnies, hear the deep grunt of a hungry pig, or feel the tremble of the ground made by the fluttering of an entire brood of anxious hens? You could probably come every week and never tire of the sights to see. Whether the farm you visit has horses, cows, chickens, pigs, sheep, goats, rabbits, dogs, or cats, there is always something exciting to experience. Spend some time "down on the farm" together.

READINGS

Early Morning in the Barn by Nancy Tufuri (Greenwillow; pb Puffin)

The rooster crows and the barnyard awakens. Three little chicks go outside to greet all the other farm animals. Even the youngest reader will enjoy the animal conversations and interactions shown in this colorful picture book.

Rosie's Walk by Pat Hutchins (Macmillan; pb Macmillan)

Rosie the hen goes out for a walk before dinner and takes the reader on a tour of the farm. A sly fox follows and tries to make Rosie his dinner, but Rosie unwittingly outwits the fox.

Old MacDonald Had A Farm by Glen Rounds, illustrator (Holiday House)

This is a unique version of this favorite children's song. Mr. Rounds adds humor with his funny illustrations and his great surprise animals.

There are many farm-related books. A few of them are ***Animals on the Farm*** by Feodor Rojankovsky (Knopf), ***My Day on the Farm*** by Chiyoko Nakatani (Crowell), ***Down on the Farm With Grover*** by Ray Sipherd (Golden Press) and ***Farmyard Sounds*** by Colin and Jacqui Hawkins (Crown).

RECITINGS

DID YOU EVER SEE A FARMYARD?
(Sung to "Did You Ever See a Lassie?")

Did you ever see a farmyard,
A farmyard, a farmyard,
Did you ever see a farmyard,
Bristling with pets?

There's kittens and chickens,
And horses and more.
Did you ever see a farmyard,
All bristling with pets?

Did you ever see a farmyard,
A farmyard, a farmyard,
Did you ever see a farmyard,
Bristling with pets?

There's puppies and guppies,
And bunnies on the run.
Did you ever see a farmyard,
All bristling with pets?

HOW'S LIFE ON THE FARM?
(Sung to "Baa, Baa, Black Sheep")

Baa, baa, black sheep,
How's life on the farm?
Do the animals get along?
Are you happy in the barn?

"Oh, yes," bleats the sheep,
"Oink, oink," agrees the pig,
"Quack, quack," says the duck,
in a voice so loud and big.

"Neigh, neigh," says the horse,
"Moo, moo," replies the cow,
"Oh, yes, we're doing fine,"
Adds the dog with a bow-wow.

Baa, baa, black sheep,
It sounds all right to me.
"Yes, I think you're right,
We all seem to agree."

RECIPES

FEED-THE-ANIMALS TREAT

Many petting zoos have ice cream cones filled with dry animal food that you can buy to feed the animals. Make your own version of this treat for your child, and pretend to be feeding one of the farm animals.

1. Make a nut mixture with any of the following ingredients: peanuts, cashews, almonds, walnuts, pecans, other nuts, raisins, dried apricots, other dried fruit, chocolate chips, or carob chips.

2. Fill an ice cream cone with some of the mixture and serve.

HAY AND STRAW

The green (hay) and yellow (straw) noodles make a pretty and delicious "farm" dish.

1. Saute 1 tablespoon finely chopped onion in 3 tablespoons margarine until golden. Add ½ pound fresh sliced mushrooms and cook for 3 minutes, stirring often.

2. Add ½ pound cooked cubed ham (or turkey) and cook 1–2 minutes.

3. Add 3 tablespoons margarine and ½ cup cream. Cook until cream thickens slightly. Salt and pepper to taste.

4. Meanwhile, cook 8 oz. fettucini noodles and 8 oz. spinach noodles according to directions on their boxes, al dente. Drain.

5. Add sauce and ½ cup grated parmesan cheese and toss. Serve immediately with ½ cup more grated parmesan to sprinkle on top.

ACTIVITIES

FARM FIELD TRIP

The most important of all is to go to a farm. Take a camera with you and enjoy the farm with your child.

THE FARMER IN THE DELL

This old favorite singing game can be played with a group of family members and/or friends. One player is chosen to be the farmer, and the others form a circle with the farmer in the middle. They hold hands and march around the farmer singing...

> The farmer in the dell,
> The farmer in the dell,
> Heigh-ho, the derry-o,
> The farmer in the dell.

The farmer chooses a player from the circle to step inside with him to be his wife. The others march around again and sing:

> The farmer takes a wife,
> The farmer takes a wife,
> Heigh-ho, the derry-o,
> The farmer takes a wife.

As each of the next verses is sung, another player is chosen by the one just picked, and joins the growing crowd in the middle.

> The wife takes a child, *etc.*
> The child takes the dog, *etc.*
> The dog takes the cat, *etc.*
> The cat takes the rat, *etc.*
> The rat takes the cheese, *etc.*
> The cheese stands alone.

Everyone stands in her place and claps her hands while all sing the last verse. The cheese then becomes the farmer for the next game. If there's only you and your child to play, arrange her stuffed animals in a circle, and have her bring them in as you sing the verses.

QUILL PEN

If you happen to find a goose feather while at the farm, bring it home to use as a quill pen. Cut the tip of the quill at an angle with a very sharp knife. Dip it in paint and draw with it. You may even wish to dip the feather part into the paint to see what kind of design it makes on the paper.

TOY FARMYARD

Choose a shallow box to be your farmyard. Cover the bottom with sand. Choose some or all of the following ideas to embellish your farmyard.

■ Use a small mirror as a duck pond.

■ Dip pieces of sponge in green ink, stick them on toothpicks, and use them as trees.

■ Cut out barns and farm animals from stiff paper, color them, and mount them on small blocks of wood. If you already have some toy animals, use those!

■ Use a strip of moss for grass.

This kind of creative, open-ended toy is one you will probably use over and over again.

96

FOURTH WEEK

Strawberries

Little freckles all around
Topped off with a frilled green crown.

Strawberry jam, strawberry shortcake, strawberry ice cream, strawberry pancakes, strawberry pie—all these delectable treats come in June when strawberry season peaks. Most everyone enjoys the summer-fresh taste of strawberries; many preserve this special taste for dreary winter days by freezing berries now. But other than eating them, what fun can a two or three year old have with strawberries? Plenty! Read on to get some "berry" good ideas for summertime strawberry fun.

READINGS

Jamberry by Bruce Degan (Harper Junior Books; pb Harper Junior Books)

This delightful book is brim full of berry rhymes, playful berry pictures, and thoroughly enjoyable berry fun. Your mouth will water as you read about the berrying adventures of a boy and a bear.

The Big Hungry Bear by Don and Audrey Wood (Playspaces)

When a little mouse spies a red, ripe strawberry, his problems begin. There's only one way to save a red, ripe strawberry from a big hungry bear—and he has to find it out quickly! This is an enchanting story.

Max's Breakfast by Rosemary Wells (Dial Books for Young Readers)

Max's sister Ruby won't let him eat his strawberries unless he eats his eggs first. As usual, Max comes up with a clever solution.

RECITINGS

POP, GO THE BERRIES
(sung to "Pop, Goes the Weasel")

All around the strawberry fields,
We picked some juicy berries.
We brought them home and washed them
    off.
Pop! go the berries!
(Open mouth as if to pop berries in.)

(KYLE) AND JILL
(sung to "Jack and Jill")

(Kyle) and Jill
Went to the field,
To fetch a bunch of berries.
(Kyle) fell down,
Berries all around,
So Jill had less to carry!

RECIPES

You probably already have many wonderful "adult" strawberry recipes, so here are several "children's" (easy-to-make) recipes to share with your child.

STRAWBERRY SQUASH

1. Give your child a strawberry, and have him wash it and remove its stem. Then let him squash it with a fork on a plate.

2. To make a great-tasting sandwich, toast 2 pieces of whole wheat bread, spread peanut butter on one slice, then top it with the strawberry squash. Put the other piece of toast on top, and you have a nutritious peanut butter-strawberry "squash" sandwich!

STRAWBERRY MILKSHAKE

1. Blend together 1 cup milk, ½ sliced ripe banana, and 3–5 stemmed strawberries.

2. Add ¼ cup wheat germ and blend till smooth to make an especially nutritious breakfast drink.

ACTIVITIES

STRAWBERRY PICKING

The first and most obvious activity to consider is to go strawberry picking with your child if there are fields near where you live. Only you can decide if your child is ready for this kind of activity. Even if you go to a local field for ten minutes, it will be worth it to let your child see how strawberries grow, how they are picked, and how they taste fresh from the patch. You might end up with only ten berries in your basket (and ten berries in your child's tummy), but you can buy some at the stand to bring home for later treats.

STRAWBERRY PRINTS

Take a fresh, firm strawberry and cut it in half. Give your child some white paper and let her make strawberry prints by pressing the strawberry half down on the paper to leave an imprint. If your child wants to change the shape of the print, have her take a bite out of the strawberry, print with it and see what it looks like then. After the prints dry, add designs with crayons or markers to incorporate the prints into pictures.

STRAWBERRY PEOPLE

Give your child a small bowl of various sized strawberries, several toothpicks, an orange with a slice cut from the bottom so it will stand without rolling, and some peanut butter to use for glue. Let him be as creative as he likes in making people and designs with the strawberries. For example, three strawberries stacked on top of each other on a toothpick can be the beginning of a strawberry snowman. (Watch carefully, of course, so your child doesn't get in trouble with the toothpick.)

98

JULY

Freedom Treasures

July is a time to celebrate freedoms: freedom as symbolized by a graceful floating balloon; freedom from routine eating as people head outdoors for picnics and find summertime treats to eat; the freedom of running along a beach or lake shore and playing in the sand; and the freedom of America as celebrated on the Fourth of July.

The activities in this chapter all deal with the wonderful treasures afforded us by summertime. Enjoy them with your little one.

FIRST WEEK

America

My country, 'tis of thee,
Sweet land of liberty,
Of thee I sing.
Land where my fathers died,
Land of the pilgrims' pride,
From every mountainside,
Let freedom ring!

Birthdays are times of celebration and joy. A child's birthday is probably her favorite day of the entire year—and it should be, for it's a day on which she's recognized and showered with attention. Everything that day is special just for her.

The Fourth of July is our country's birthday, and it's traditionally a day of celebration and joy, too—a day when our country is recognized and showered with attention, and everything is made special in honor of her. It is a day of flags, balloons, picnics, fireworks, and parades.

However you choose to celebrate the Fourth of July, bring some special meaning to it for your child by explaining it as America's birthday. Plan a "birthday party" for America in your own unique way. Below are some ideas of things you might do.

READINGS

Parade by Donald Crews (Greenwillow; pb Morrow)

Colorful, bold illustrations with appropriate words and phrases bring this picturebook parade to life. Donald Crews treats his readers to a parade that includes everyone from the balloon-seller and the ice cream vendor to the fire trucks and the street cleaner.

America's Birthday—the Fourth of July by Tom Shachtman (Macmillan)

Although this book is marketed for older children, the photographs are an excellent chronicle of America's birthday. Share just the photographs with your child.

Summer Snowman by Gene Zion (Harper & Row)

What could be a bigger hit on the Fourth of July than the grand fireworks display? Little Henry comes up with something in this funny story. Though it may be a bit long for some twos and threes, this story is so satisfying and refreshing that you may wish to give it a try.

RECITINGS

RED, WHITE, AND BLUE
(Sung to "Three Blind Mice")

Red, white, and blue,
Red, white, and blue,
Three colors so true,
Three colors so true.
They are the colors of my country,
A wonderful country because we are free,
Three colors that mean so much to me,
Red, white, and blue.

America
(Sung to "The Muffin Man")

Do you know America,
America, America?
Do you know America,
The country where we live?

Yes, I know America,
America, America.
Yes, I know America,
The country where we live.

We all love our country,
Yes, we do, yes, we do.
We all love our country,
For the freedoms that it gives.

July Fourth is its birthday,
Its birthday, its birthday.
July Fourth is its birthday,
So we will celebrate.

We'll have parades and fireworks,
Fireworks, fireworks.
We'll have parades and fireworks,
Because it is so great!

RECIPES

RED, WHITE, AND BLUE BERRIES

1. Wash some strawberries and blueberries, and then mash them very lightly with a fork.

2. Mix them into vanilla yogurt in serving-size dishes.

3. You may wish to sprinkle some coconut on the top.

AMERICAN FLAG COOKIES

1. In a large mixing bowl, beat together ½ cup margarine and ½ cup shortening. Add ¼ cup white sugar and ¼ cup brown sugar. Beat till fluffy.

2. Add 1 egg, 2 tablespoons milk, and 1 teaspoon vanilla. Beat well.

3. Gradually add 2 cups flour, ¼ cup wheat germ, ½ teaspoon baking soda, and ¼ teaspoon salt.

4. Divide the dough in half. To one half, add several drops of red food coloring and stir until well mixed.

5. Layer the dough as follows: Put a piece of waxed paper in the bottom and up two sides of an 8" x 4" x 2" loaf pan. Press half of the red dough evenly in the pan. Top with half of the plain dough, patting evenly. Repeat red and plain layers, patting each evenly. Cover and chill at least 4 hours.

6. Turn oven to 375°.

7. Grasp the waxed paper to lift the dough out of the pan. With a sharp knife, slice the dough crosswise into three equal parts. Cut each of these three sections into ¼" slices, getting about twelve from each section.

8. Place slices 1" apart on ungreased cookie sheets. Bake for 8–10 minutes or till edges are golden.

9. In upper left corner of each flag, spread a 1" square of blue frosting. Decorate with sugar or white decorator icing to make the stars. Makes about 36 cookies.

ACTIVITIES

AMERICAN STREAMER FLAG

Tape two-foot lengths of red, white, and blue crepe paper streamers to a stick; have your child wave it in the breeze.

FIREWORKS DISPLAY

Crumple several pieces of colored tissue paper and glue them in a small circle in the center of a piece of black construction paper. "Draw" lines with glue going out from the tissue paper circle. Cover the glue with glitter. Shake off the excess glitter. You'll have a fireworks picture bursting right in front of you!

LIBERTY BELL RING

Hang a bell up high and securely. Have your child toss beanbags up at the bell to make it ring.

FOURTH OF JULY PARADE

Orchestrate your own Fourth of July Parade. Have your child play a homemade instrument (such as a cooking-pot drum) or carry an American flag or the streamer flag above. Sing the following version of Yankee Doodle as you march along.

YANKEE DOODLE

Yankee Doodle went to town,
A-riding on a pony,
Stuck a feather in his cap
And called it macaroni!

We will march around today,
And have a celebration,
We'll sing for our America
To honor our great nation!

Yankee Doodle, keep it up,
Yankee Doodle clever.
Our country's such a special place
We'll love it now and forever.

Pancake Day

Great A, little a,
This is pancake day;
Toss the ball high,
Throw the ball low,
Those that come after
May sing heigh-ho!

A stack of pancakes hot off the griddle with a dollop of butter and a trickle of maple syrup is enough to make any mouth water! Pancakes are a favorite breakfast treat for young and old alike. Why? It might be because they're an acceptable excuse to indulge in maple syrup, but I think it's more than that.

From the cook's point of view, pancakes are wonderfully versatile. They can take on any shape, from a teddy bear to the Statue of Liberty. They can take on any flavor, from strawberry to granola. They can be enjoyed any time of day, from breakfast to midnight snack. And they will be enjoyed *any* time of the year. Whatever *your* reasons for enjoying them, do!

READINGS

Pancakes for Breakfast by Tomie dePaola (Harcourt, Brace, Jovanovich)

When a little old lady tries to make herself some pancakes for breakfast in this wordless book, she encounters amusing obstacles. She overcomes them all and, in the process, demonstrates the importance of trying again if you don't succeed at first.

The Pancake Boy by Lorinda Bryan Cauley (Putnam)

This old Norwegian folk tale is a long but most enjoyable adventure of a pancake who tries to escape the inevitable.

Little Bear's Pancake Party by Janice Brustlein (Lothrop, Lee & Shepard Co.)

It is spring and Little Bear wakes up from his long hibernation craving pancakes. When he's finally given some, he gets a surprise along with them. This story might be a bit long, but it's a cute one to try with your toddler.

RECITINGS

TEN LITTLE PANCAKES
(Sung to "Ten Little Indians")

One little, two little, three little pancakes,
Four little, five little, six little pancakes,
Seven little, eight little, nine little pancakes,
Ten pancakes ready to eat.

Three pancakes speckled with red strawberries,
Three pancakes dotted with ripe blueberries,
Four pancakes sprinkled with wild blackberries,
Ten pancakes ready to eat.

Ten little, nine little, eight little pancakes,
Seven little, six little, five little pancakes,
Four little, three little, two little pancakes,
One pancake left to eat.

I can't believe I ate ten pancakes,
I'm so full, I have a tummy ache,
Next time I'll try not to eat all that I make,
Ten were too much for me!

STIR, STIR, STIR
(Sung to "Row, Row, Row Your Boat")

Stir, stir, stir it up,
Pancakes are a treat.
I like to mix the batter up,
But mostly love to eat!

RECIPES

BASIC PANCAKES

1. Sift together 2 cups flour (any combination of white, whole wheat, rye, oat, buckwheat, or wheat germ), 2 teaspoons baking powder, 3 tablespoons brown or white sugar, and ½ teaspoon salt.

2. Beat three eggs lightly.

3. Pour eggs and 2 cups milk into flour mixture.

4. Mix only long enough to blend. Batter should be lumpy.

5. Stir in 3 tablespoons oil or melted butter.

6. Cook on a hot griddle. Makes 12 large pancakes.

ANIMAL PANCAKES

1. Stir together ¾ cup all-purpose flour, ¼ cup wheat germ, 1-½ teaspoons baking powder, ½ teaspoon sugar, and a pinch of salt.

2. Break 1 egg into a bowl and add 1 cup milk and 2 tablespoons oil. Whisk together very well.

3. Pour the egg mixture into the flour mixture and whisk until the batter is quite smooth and has almost no lumps.

4. Melt a small amount of butter on the griddle or in the frying pan you will be using.

5. To make a teddy bear pancake: spoon 1 tablespoon of batter into the pan (or onto the griddle) for the body and then add 1 teaspoon above the body for the head. With another teaspoon of the batter make the ears, hands and feet. Make as many pancakes in this fashion as you can without them touching one another.

6. Cook the pancakes over medium heat.

7. To make a giraffe pancake: spoon 1 tablespoon of batter for the body and then add 1 teaspoon in a line coming out from the upper left side for the neck. Add ½ teaspoon of batter at the top of the neck for the giraffe's head. Add four long thin legs and a little tail in the appropriate places with about ½ teaspoon for each leg and ¼ teaspoon for the tail.

See if you can use this technique to make the animal your child loves the most.

PANCAKE CREATIVITY

No matter what kind of batter you use, you can add your own little touches to each pancake. Some examples include adding fresh, sliced strawberries; sliced or mashed bananas, blueberries, peaches, apples or any other fruit you might like; or raisins, chopped nuts, coconut, or cinnamon. You might let your child put her own special ingredients into her pancake, if you think it's something the two of you can handle safely.

104

ACTIVITIES

PANCAKE MATCHING GAME

Make a set of pancake cards for a matching game to play with your child. Make two of each design you choose. Blueberry pancakes might be round with three blue dots colored in; strawberry pancakes might be oval with two strawberry slices in each. Lay the cards out on a table and have your child find the matching pairs. You could also play a simple card game with them if your child is mature enough.

PANCAKE THEATRICS

The story of **Pancakes for Breakfast** is a great one to act out. Your child can be the little lady who tries to make herself pancakes for breakfast, and you can be the various animals that interact with her—or you might choose to be the little lady and let your child act out the animal roles. In either case, the most exciting part is the end when the pancakes are actually consumed! You might want to make *that* part real.

CHURNING BUTTER

In the **Pancakes for Breakfast** story, the little lady has to churn her own butter. You might like to do this experiment with your child to teach him where butter comes from:

Put 2 cups of heavy cream into a clear plastic container with a lid. Add one clean marble. Cover tightly and shake. (The marble acts like the dasher of a churn.) In about fifteen minutes, the butter should separate from the thin, white liquid (buttermilk). Press out all the liquid with a wooden spoon. Remove the marble. Chill the butter; add a pinch of salt if desired.

105

The Balloon

"What is the news of the day,
Good neighbor, I pray?"
"They say the balloon
Is gone up to the moon!"

Have you ever gone to a parade or carnival and not seen bouquets of colorful balloons? Have you ever celebrated a child's birthday without decorations of streamers and balloons? Have you ever known a child whose eyes don't sparkle at the sight of a balloon?

Balloons are great toys because of all they can do and be. They can be blown up, let go, bounced, thrown, caught, flown, and popped—for starters. They are lightweight balls for all kinds of sports, decorations for all kinds of parties, and bearers of happiness for all kinds of occasions.

A package of balloons is one "toy" every household with children (aged two and older, or past the stage where every object goes straight to the mouth) should have on hand. Balloons can provide hours of enjoyment. So take time out to have some "light-hearted" balloon fun.

(Please do be very carful using balloons with young children. A popped or uninflated balloon can cause choking if it's accidentally inhaled. Supervise balloon play closely, and be safe.)

READINGS

A Balloon For Grandad by Nigel Gray (Orchard Books)

Sam's special balloon escapes out the back door, and Sam is very sad until he and his dad fantasize that the wind might be taking the balloon to North Africa where Sam's grandfather lives.

Benjamin's Balloon by Janet Quin-Harkin (Parent's Magazine)

When Benjamin finds a balloon on the lawn one morning and blows it up, his adventure begins. As it gets bigger and bigger, he seems to get in more and more trouble. Finally he takes to the sky, and then he can't find a way to get back down. He eventually does, of course, and the reader will be as content at the end of the story as Benjamin was.

Georgie and the Runaway Balloon by Robert Bright (Doubleday)

The little ghost Georgie and his friends go to the country fair, where Herman the cat buys a balloon. The adventure begins when a mouse unties the balloon from Herman's tail. Georgie saves the day in his usual clever way.

RECITINGS

BALLOONS
(Sung to "Row, Row, Row Your Boat")

Red, green, yellow, blue,
Floating in the air.
Balloons so light and graceful,
Playing here and there.

Big, small, round, and fat,
Every shape and size.

Balloons are such exciting toys,
And such a great surprise.

WHERE HAS MY BLUE BALLOON GONE?
(Sung to "Where, Oh, Where Has My Little Dog Gone?")

Where, oh, where has my blue balloon gone?
Oh, where, oh, where can it be?
Daddy bought it for me just five minutes ago,
Oh, where, oh, where can it be?

I was so glad when Dad gave it to me.
I've always wanted one blue.
I grabbed the string but it slipped right
    through.
Oh, what, oh, what did I do?

I watched it as it rose into the sky,
I watched it fly out of sight.
It's gone, I'm sad, but now I've learned,
And next time I'll hold on tight!

RECIPES

BALLOON SANDWICHES
Fill any round roll (such as a hamburger bun or bagel) with the following delicious chicken salad or another sandwich filling your child likes. Put it on a plate and attach a piece of cooked spaghetti for the balloon's string. Serve with cherry tomatoes, cucumber rounds, and carrot slices on the side.

SPECIAL CHICKEN SALAD
1. Combine 2 cups cooked and diced chicken; 1 cup unsweetened pineapple tidbits, drained, (reserve juice); 1 cup seedless green grapes cut in half; ½ cup chopped celery; ⅔ cup peanuts.

2. Combine ¼ cup mayonnaise, ¼ cup plain yogurt, 2 tablespoons pineapple juice.

3. Fold into first mixture. Makes 12 servings.

BALLOON CAKE
1. Make a favorite cake recipe or a box cake in an oblong pan, 13" x 9" x 2". Frost with the Butter Cream Frosting below. Decorate by arranging pastel mint wafers for balloons in a cluster in the upper corner of the cake. Use shoestring licorice for balloon strings; bring all the strings to one point in the lower corner of the cake.

BUTTER CREAM FROSTING
1. Blend ⅓ cup margarine and 3 cups confectioners' sugar.

2. Stir in 1-½ teaspoons vanilla and about 2 tablespoons milk. Beat until smooth and of spreading consistency.

ACTIVITIES

BALLOON GAMES
There are many physical activities for which balloons are wonderful. You can play balloon soccer, balloon catch, balloon volleyball, balloon badminton, or balloon toss (where the child tries to toss the balloon into a large box or laundry basket).

WATER BALLOONS
On a hot summer day, why not fill some balloons with water, put on bathing suits, and play water-balloon bowling. Set up a tower of blocks for your child to roll her balloon toward. See if she can knock them down without bursting the balloon. When a balloon does break, pick up the pieces immediately and dispose of them.

DECORATED BALLOONS
Give your child an inflated balloon and a permanent marking pen. Have him decorate the balloon as a face, or however else he wishes.

FOURTH WEEK

Picnics

Going on a picnic
Leaving right away.
If it doesn't rain
We'll stay all day.

Summertime is often synonymous with outdoor-time. Outdoor activities are plentiful, with beaches, biking, tennis, hiking, boating, fishing, swinging, camping, and swimming. Even eating takes to the outdoors, with summertime picnics supplying natural entertainment. A picnic can be as spontaneous as picking up your lunch and walking outdoors with it to enjoy the fresh air or as elaborate as a planned family reunion complete with traditional family recipes and organized games. However your picnics shape up, do spend some summer time picnicking with your child. It's a special treat no one should miss.

READINGS

Having a Picnic by Sarah Garland (Atlantic Monthly Press)

Mommy takes her two daughters on a frolicking picnic. The simple wording and realistic illustrations make this an enjoyable book.

Spot's First Picnic by Eric Hill (G.P. Putnam's Sons)

In this book, the first in a new Spot series (Spot Storybooks), Spot goes on a picnic with his friends. Their adventures are comical; the ending is perfect.

Picnic by Emily Arnold McCully (Harper & Row Junior Books; pb Harper & Row Junior Books)

When a mouse family decides to go on a picnic, they all pile into their old red truck and go bumping down the road. Everyone seems to be having a great time until they realize one baby mouse is missing. All ends well in this wordless book filled with great watercolor pictures.

RECITINGS

HERE WE GO ON A PICNIC TODAY
(Sung to "The Mulberry Bush")

Here we go on a picnic today,
A picnic today, a picnic today.
Here we go on a picnic today,
On such a beautiful (Sunday.)

This is the way we pack our lunch,
Pack our lunch, pack our lunch.
This is the way we pack our lunch
On such a beautiful (Sunday.)

First we put in the sandwiches,
The sandwiches, the sandwiches.
First we put in the sandwiches
On such a beautiful (Sunday.)

Continue on in this same fashion, adding other items you'll take on your picnic.

A FILLED–UP PICNIC BASKET
(Sung to "A Tisket, A Tasket")

A tisket, a tasket, a filled-up picnic basket.
Mom's stuffed it with such yummy treats,
I can't wait to unpack it.

Unpack it, unpack it,
I can't wait to unpack it.
Crackers, cheese, and fresh fruit, please,
Kept safe tucked in our basket.

Our basket, our basket,
There's more things in our basket.
Juice and bars and my toy cars
To play with—let's unpack it!

RECIPES

POCKET PICNIC

Pockets are indispensable to a toddler, for they are where all their "treasures" can go. And toddlers are always collecting treasures—pebbles, paper clips, shells, dead bugs, pennies, raisins, and anything else that catches their eyes. So plan a picnic filled with pockets. First, make sure you and your child wear clothing with plenty of pockets. In your own pockets, hide little treasures like balloons, stickers, small bottles of bubbles, little toys, and any other special treats your child would enjoy playing with. Take them out whenever you want to surprise her. For food, make Pocket Sandwiches and Pocket Cookies.

POCKET SANDWICHES

Not only are these fun for kids who love pockets, but they're a neat way to eat, too. Fill pocket bread (pita) with your child's favorite sandwich filling. Stuff them as full as you'd like, and then close them up until you are ready to eat.

POCKET COOKIES

1. In a mixing bowl, beat together ½ cup margarine, ½ cup shortening, and ½ cup sugar. Add 1 egg, 1 tablespoon milk, and ½ teaspoon vanilla.

2. Gradually add 2-¼ cups flour, ½ teaspoon baking soda, and ¼ teaspoon salt. Beat till well mixed.

3. Divide the dough in half. Shape each half into a roll 3" in diameter. Wrap them in clear plastic and chill for at least six hours. (If the dough is too soft to shape into rolls, put it in the freezer for about thirty minutes, and try again.)

4. When you want to bake the cookies, preheat the oven to 375°. Unwrap the rolls of dough and cut them into ⅛" slices. You should get about 16 slices from each roll.

5. Place half the slices on an ungreased cookie sheet about 2" apart. Place 2 teaspoons of a filling (see below) in the center of each circle, then top each with a plain circle of dough. Press a floured fork around the edges to seal well.

6. Bake for 12–15 minutes.

7. Fillings: peanut butter, jelly, raisins, coconut, chocolate chips, chopped nuts, or any flavor pie filling.

ACTIVITIES

PICNIC FOLLOW–THE–LEADER

Any indoor game or activity takes on a new shine outdoors. Try Follow the Leader at your picnic. Be as creative as you feel. Have your child crawl like an ant, make a trail around trees, under bushes and picnic tables.

PICNIC TREASURE HUNT

Every child loves treasure hunts. An outdoors one will be extra special. Hide peanuts or other such items for your child to find. See how many things your child can stuff into her pocket. (Be sure to hide the objects in obvious places!)

FEED THE ANTS

After you've finished eating, why not conduct a live science experiment and feed the ants rather than throw the crumbs away? Find a mound of sand or dirt where ants are living. Have your child drop some tiny crumbs of bread or other leftovers on it and watch what happens. Where do they go? How do they carry the food? See how much you can learn just from careful observation.

NATURAL ENTERTAINMENT

Nature will supply your entertainment. You can watch the clouds in the sky, play in the sand, take nature walks, listen for sounds of birds and bees, make sound with grass blades, play tag, the list goes on and on! Bring a few balls, perhaps a Nerf frisbee, and you and your child will be content for hours.

FIFTH WEEK

By the Sea

By the sea, by the sea
By the beautiful sea.
You and me, you and me,
Oh, how happy we'll be!

A day at the beach to a child means building sand castles, swimming, collecting shells and pebbles, eating snacks of ice cream and candy, and getting sunburned. Add to that the benefits of the fresh air, good healthy exercise, and all-day entertainment, and you'll wonder why you aren't there right now! Where else could you have so much summertime fun with your little one? So, pack the necessary clothes, toys, and goodies and head out for your favorite beach or lake or riverfront.

READINGS

Miffy at the Beach by Dick Bruna (Price Stern)

The reader will share in the fun as Miffy and her daddy, Mr. Rabbit, spend a wonderful day at the beach together building sand castles, collecting shells, and swimming in the cold water.

Jack Goes To The Beach by Jill Krementz (Random)

In this Big Board Book, the reader goes with Jack to the beach for the day. The real photographs make you feel as if you were right there.

On My Beach There Are Many Pebbles by Leo Lionni (Astor-Honor, Inc.)

This very clever book will encourage the reader to be creative with pebbles. This is a great follow-up book after having been to the beach.

RECITINGS

WE'RE GOING TO THE BEACH
(Sung to "The Farmer in the Dell")

We're going to the beach,
We're going to the beach.
Heigh-ho, the derry-o,
We're going to the beach.

We're going to build in sand
We're going to build in sand.
Heigh-ho, the derry-o,
We're going to build in sand.

Add other verses as you wish.
We're going to collect some shells, *etc.*
We're going to splash and swim, *etc.*

AT THE BEACH
(Sung to "Yankee Doodle")

(Matthew Brennan) went to the beach,
Along with his whole family.
They played in sand and water,
And were so very happy.

At the beach, there's lots to do,
In sand and sea and sun.

111

Take some time, enjoy the view,
You'll have a lot of fun.

Here are two cookie recipes using summery ingredients. Both can be packed and taken to the beach or the lake. Add some fruit and some juice, and you'll be well-equipped with beach treats.

LEMONADE COOKIES

1. Preheat oven to 375°.

2. Beat together 1 cup margarine and ½ cup sugar till fluffy.

3. Beat in 2 eggs.

4. In medium mixing bowl, stir together 2-½ cups flour, ½ cup wheat germ, and 1 teaspoon baking soda. Add half this mixture to the margarine mixture and beat well.

5. Beat in ½ cup lemonade concentrate and then the remaining flour mixture. Mix well.

6. Drop by rounded teaspoons about 2" apart onto greased cookie sheets.

7. Bake for 10–12 minutes. Cool for 10 minutes. Makes about 60 cookies.

POTATO CHIP CRUNCHIES

1. Preheat oven to 350°.

2. Beat 1 cup margarine with ½ cup sugar and 2 teaspoons vanilla.

3. Gradually add 2 cups flour and 1 cup crushed potato chips, beating till well mixed.

4. Drop by rounded teaspoons about 2" apart onto ungreased cookie sheets. Flatten the dough with a wet fork that has been dipped in sugar.

5. Bake for 12–15 minutes. Makes 36 cookies.

BEACH SCENES

Spread some glue on a piece of construction paper either in a pattern or along the bottom edge. Give your child some sand to sprinkle onto the paper so it will stick wherever the glue is. Once it's set, add shells, tissue paper, or other decorations to the beach scene. You might also like to do this in a shoe box and make a beach diorama out of it.

SAND COMB

Make a sand comb by cutting notches along one side of a piece of heavy cardboard. Then let your child use it to "comb" patterns in the sand.

SAND SCOOP

Use an empty plastic bleach bottle with its cap securely fastened to make a sand scoop. Just cut the bottom of the bottle off diagonally, and it will be ready for your child to play with at the beach.

BEACH TREASURE HUNT

There are various ways in which to have a beach treasure hunt: Name specific items for your child to try to find; hide various items for him to find; give him, one at a time, natural objects that you found on the beach (such as seaweed, a certain shape shell, a pink rock) and have him find something like them.

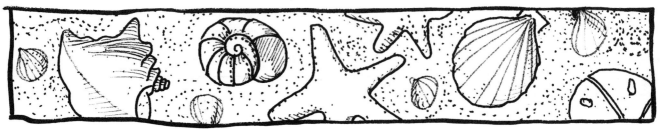

Chapter Eight

AUGUST

Treasures to Beat the Heat

August in most of the country is hot. Record-breaking temperatures and hundred-percent humidity drain away our energy. Fortunately, there are ways to beat the heat. A cool shower for you and a cool bath for your little one can do wonders to help escape the heat for a while. Going out to dinner rescues you from a hot, steamy kitchen. Going to a lake on an early morning fishing trip will be fun and breezy. Even sitting and listening to the sounds around you can be fun on a late-summer day.

All these treasures to help you beat the heat are discussed in this chapter. Try a few, and see if you and your little one can stay cool.

FIRST WEEK

Rub-a-dub-dub

Rub-a-dub-dub, three men in a tub,
And who do you think they be?
The butcher, the baker, the candlestick maker—
Turn them out, knaves all three!

Do children enjoy getting dirty for its own sake, or is it so they can take a bath? It's probably a little of both! A child's bath means far more to him than merely cleaning up: it means a time to play in the water. Whether your child steps into his bath with boats or bubbles or ladles and measuring cups and spoons, he's stepping into a water playground. As he plays, he's experimenting with water and what it does. Try to allow plenty of bath time for your child to be immersed in the fun and experimentation of water. Below are listed some common water toys as well as some new ideas for you to offer as your child enjoys bath time.

READINGS

Sam's Bath by Barbro Lindgren (Morrow)
Sam proves through a series of silly events that a bath is a fun experience—even for his dog! This is one of a series of Sam books that show Sam involved in various comical learning situations. The others are ***Sam's Ball***, ***Sam's Cookie***, ***Sam's Teddy Bear***, ***Sam's Potty***, ***Sam's Wagon***, ***Sam's Car***, and ***Sam's Lamp***.

Bathtime by Maureen Roffey (Macmillan)
Simple questions lead toddlers to talk about bath routines in this bright picture book.

The Case of the Missing Duckie by Linda Hayward (Western Publishing Group)
Ernie is all set to take a bath, but something is missing—his rubber duckie—and he certainly cannot take a bath without his duck. Ernie goes on a search, enlists the help of Sherlock Hemlock, and eventually finds him.

RECITINGS

ROW, ROW, ROW YOUR BOAT

Row, row, row your boat
Gently down the stream.
Merrily, merrily, merrily, merrily,
Life is but a dream.

This is a good bathtub song. You may wish to add verses of your own, like these.

Clean, clean, clean yourself,
From your head down to your toes.
Wash away the caked-on mud,
Down the drain it goes!

Splash, splash, splash around,
Baths are fun times, too.
Play with toys, make some noise,
Play a game that's new.

MY BATH
(Sung to "My Bonnie Lies Over the Ocean")

My two feet step into the bathtub,
My two knees bend so I can sit,
My bottom sits down in the water,
BRRR—it's cold—I don't like this one bit!

Turn on, turn on,
Oh, turn on more hot water, please, oh please,
Turn on, turn on,
Oh, turn on more hot water, please.

The water is getting much warmer,
It feels almost perfect to me.
I look for my toys to start playing,
I grab every one that I see.

Playtime, playtime,
Oh, bath time is playtime for me, for me.
Playtime, playtime,
Oh, bath time is playtime for me.

I've been in the water so long now,
My mommy says time to get out.
If I stay for just one more second,
She fears I'll turn into a trout!

Get out, get out,
Come wrap in this towel warm and dry.
Get out, get out,
Bath's done—time to say good-bye.

RECIPES

SINKING/FLOATING JELLO

Experiment with sinking and floating, using food.

1. Prepare one recipe of gelatin, using a package of fruit-flavored Jell-O or one envelope of Knox gelatin with 2 cups of fruit juice. If possible, use a clear bowl.

2. When the gelatin is cool but still liquid, add some or all of the following: blueberries, sliced banana, sliced peaches, sliced or whole strawberries, grated coconut, grated carrot, chopped walnuts, crushed pineapple. (You and your child may think of other ingredients you'd like to add.)

3. Have your child watch while some things sink and others float. Talk about them.

4. Chill the jello and eat the layered treat!

FIZZY APPLE DRINK

Bubbles fascinate children. Make this refreshing drink, and let your child study these bubbles.

1. Cut one apple in quarters.

2. Put three ice cubes in each of four tall glasses. Pour 1 cup of apple juice and then ½ cup of club soda or seltzer water into each glass. Add one apple quarter to each glass, and serve right away.

ACTIVITIES

TUB TOYS

Here are some obvious and some not-so-obvious ideas about things to take into the tub: measuring cups and spoons, sponges, corks, plastic tubing, straws, a shower hose, washcloths, egg beater, meat baster, ladle, eye dropper, ping-pong balls or other small balls, watering can, strainer, plastic squeeze bottle, spray pump bottles, boats, soaps, and bubbles. The most important tub toy is one you can't

supply—it's your child's imagination, and he will definitely bring it along!

SINKING AND FLOATING

Make a collection of objects your child can use to experiment with sinking and floating. Some ideas: comb, paper, toothbrush, aluminum foil, crayon, sock, cotton swab, cup, spoon.

WATER LENS

Make a water lens your child can use to look at objects under bath water covered with bubbles. Cut the bottom out of a plastic pail. Stretch plastic wrap over the top of the pail and fasten it with a rubber band. Put the end with the plastic wrap into the water. When she looks through the open bottom, your child should be able to see what's underneath the bubbles.

BUBBLES, BUBBLES, BUBBLES!

One of the nicest things about baths is the opportunity to play with bubbles. Here are two recipes for homemade bubbles for blowing.

■ Mix ¼ cup liquid detergent, ½ cup water, a few drops food coloring, and 1 teaspoon sugar.

■ Mix ½ cup liquid detergent, a few drops salad oil, 2 tablespoons water, and a few drops food coloring.

For a wand, use a pipe cleaner shaped with a loop at one end to dip into the bubble solution.

Pease Porridge

Pease porridge hot, pease porridge cold,
Pease porridge in the pot
Nine days old.
Some like it hot, some like it cold,
Some like it in the pot
Nine days old.

During the summer, families tend to eat out more often. It may be because of family vacations or because hot kitchens are no fun in August, but whatever the reasons, restaurants seem to be busier.

Eating out with your child can be a thoroughly enjoyable and enriching experience for you all if you plan ahead and go prepared. There are three general rules to help assure a more relaxing time. First, go early so you'll beat the crowds and not have too long to wait. Second, bring some finger-food appetizers in case your little one gets too hungry too soon. And third, bring some toys to pass the time as you wait for your food to be served.

The activities below will help you plan ahead for a pleasant time at a restaurant.

READINGS

Benjy Goes to a Restaurant by Jill Krementz (Crown)

This photographic board book is a great one that shows a little boy dining out with Mom and Dad. Everyone in the family will enjoy this positive book.

Frog Goes to Dinner by Mercer Mayer (Dial Books for Young Readers; pb Dial Books for Young Readers)

When Frog secretly joins the family on their outing to a posh restaurant, everyone is in for a surprise! This wordless picture book cleverly tells a wonderfully funny story.

Eating Out by Helen Oxenbury (Dial Books for Young Readers)

When Mom is too tired to cook, a family of three goes out for dinner. They seem to find going out with their toddler even more exhausting than cooking and eating at home in this comic look at dining out with children.

RECITINGS

SIT AROUND THE TABLE
(Sung to "Ring Around A Rosy")

Sit around the table,
As patient as I'm able,
We've ordered food,
I must be good,
And wait if I am able.

Mom's got some toys to play with,
Dad has a story to say with
Some funny rhymes and silly lines
To pass the time away with.

I see the waiter coming,
He smiles at me—he's humming.
He brings our food,
Says I've been good,
It really was nothing!

WHAT'S YOUR FAVORITE FOOD TO EAT?

(Sung to "London Bridge")

What's your favorite food to eat,
Food to eat, food to eat?
What's your favorite food to eat,
My dear (Maggie)?

Pizza pie with lots of cheese,
Lots of cheese, lots of cheese.
Pizza pie with lots of cheese,
My dear Mommy.

Add other verses that fit your child's likings.
Ice cream cones with sprinkles on top, *etc.*
Chocolate cookies with lots of nuts, *etc.*

RECIPES

The following appetizer snacks can be made ahead and taken along when you go out to eat. You may be glad to have them while you wait for your food to be served.

PRETZELS

1. Preheat oven to 425°.
2. Mix 1-½ cups warm (110–115°) water, 1 tablespoon yeast, and 1 tablespoon sugar together. Set aside for 5 minutes.
3. Mix 4 cups flour and 1 teaspoon salt in a bowl.
4. Add yeast mixture to the flour mixture; mix to form a dough.
5. Shape dough into classic pretzel knots or whatever other shapes you wish.
6. Brush 1 beaten egg onto pretzels. Sprinkle on coarse salt, if desired.
7. Bake for 12 minutes.

SKINNY CRACKERS

1. Preheat oven to 350°.
2. Mix ½ cup flour and 2 tablespoons sesame seeds.
3. Cut in 3 tablespoons cold butter until the mixture is crumbly.

4. Sprinkle 2 tablespoons ice water over the flour mixture.
5. Mix to form a ball.
6. Roll skinny snakes. Help your child form different shapes, animals, or his initials. Flatten a bit on ungreased cookie sheets.
7. Bake 15 minutes.

ACTIVITIES

RESTAURANT BAG

Have a special "restaurant bag" all ready to go, with treats your child will enjoy to help pass the time. You may wish to prepare this bag with your child and solicit his requests for things to put in it, or you may wish to do it yourself to surprise your child with treats you've selected for him. Some suggestions include paper and crayons, favorite books, several small toy cars, or toy figures. Think of toys that would create a little quiet time for your child.

IDEAL MEAL

Discuss with your child what his "ideal" meal would be if he could have only his absolute favorites. Plan this out to the extent that you wish, and then help him design and decorate a menu that will include his favorite foods. You can either let your child have complete freedom with his food choices or you can suggest various foods from each of the four food groups.

DESIGN A PLACE MAT

Design a place mat for and with your child. You may want to draw on the place mat a place for the plate, fork, spoon, cup and napkin to help your child learn where all of these things go. After it is completely decorated, cover it with clear contact paper to preserve it forever.

118

THIRD WEEK

Fish

One, two, three-four-five,
Once I caught a fish alive;
Six, seven, eight-nine-ten,
Then I let it go again.

If someone asked you whether you like fish, how would you answer? "Why, yes, I have a big aquarium at home," or "Yes, my sons and I go fishing every Saturday morning," or "Mmm, I especially love the taste of bluefish"?

Those are three very different ways to view fish, and a child's experiences of "fish" should include all three. A small goldfish bowl with two or three goldfish is simple enough, yet exciting and educational for a child as she watches the eating and living patterns of her fish. Going fishing is a relaxing (and sometimes even rewarding) sport, a good one for parent and child to share. And fish as the main course of a meal is a healthy and tasty source of protein. You can expand and enrich your child's fish experiences with the activities suggested below.

READINGS

Fish is Fish by Leo Lionni (Pantheon; pb Knopf)

Swimmy by Leo Lionni (Pantheon; pb Knopf)

These two books present fish in a pleasant and positive way. The reader will delight in Leo Lionni's illustrations as well as in the clever dialogue and story themes.

A Fish Out of Water by Helen Palmer (Beginner)

What happens if you feed a fish too much? Well, in this book, incredible things happen to poor Otto, the overfed fish. The little boy in the story learns a difficult lesson—almost at the expense of his pet fish—but all ends well.

Where's the Fish? by Taro Gomi (William Morrow & Co., Inc.)

A bright pink fish is cleverly hidden on the pages of this book. The reader is challenged to find it.

RECITINGS

LET'S GO FISHING
(Sung to "Frère Jacques")

Let's go fishing, let's go fishing,
At the lake, at the lake.
Fishing poles and big worms, fishing poles
    and big worms,
We will take, we will take.

MY AQUARIUM
(Sung to "The Farmer in the Dell")

The goldfish in my tank,
The goldfish in my tank,
Heigh-ho, the derry-o,
The goldfish in my tank.

My goldfish has some friends,
My goldfish has some friends.
Heigh-ho, the derry-o,
My goldfish has some friends.

He has a neon fish, *etc.*
He has a red swordtail, *etc.*
He has a striped fish, *etc.*

Add other fish you may know about or have in your child's aquarium. You can draw little fish like the ones you're singing about, cut them out, attach them to straws or popsicle sticks, and have them go swimming about in the air as you sing. Finish the song with the two verses that follow.

My tank is filled with fish, *etc.*
I love to watch them swim, *etc.*

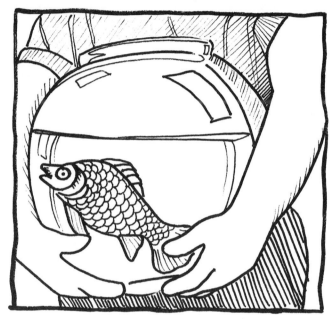

RECIPES

The simplest fishy treat is to fill a goldfish bowl with Pepperidge Farm goldfish crackers and serve them as a snack!

Some children don't especially like the taste of some fish, but there are so many tasty recipes for fish, you should be able to tempt even the most reluctant of eaters. Below is one very tasty fish dish.

FISH BURGERS

1. Add 1½ pounds of cod fillets to 1 cup boiling water. Cover and bring to a second boil. Reduce heat and cook 4 minutes or until fish flakes easily. Drain and flake. Remove any bones.

2. Mix fish with ½ cup bread crumbs, 2 tablespoons chopped parsley, ½ cup mayonnaise, ¼ cup relish, 1 egg, 1 tablespoon mustard, 1 tablespoon lemon juice, and 1 tablespoon Worchestershire sauce. Mix well.

3. Form into 12 patties about 3 inches in diameter and ¾ inches thick. Place on a greased baking sheet.

4. Bake in 400° oven for 15–20 minutes or until lightly browned. Serve on hamburger roll or English muffin, with lettuce, tomato and cheese.

FISH COOKIES

This is a great cookie recipe that can be cut out with any shape cookie cutter you wish—but for this week, make it a fish!

1. In a large mixing bowl, beat 1 cup margarine with ½ cup sugar. Beat until fluffy.

2. Add 2 tablespoons milk and 1 teaspoon vanilla. Beat well.

3. Gradually beat in 2-½ cups flour till well mixed. Mix in last part of flour with a wooden spoon or with your hands, as dough will be stiff.

4. Divide the dough into 4 parts. Wrap each part in clear plastic wrap. Chill in refrigerator for 1 to 2 hours or until firm enough to roll out.

5. Preheat oven to 375°. Remove one piece of dough from refrigerator and unwrap. On a lightly floured surface, roll out dough so it's ¼" thick. Use floured cookie cutters (fish) to cut out shapes. Place on ungreased cookie sheet. Decorate as desired (see below). Repeat with remaining dough.

6. Bake about 8 minutes. Cool for 1 minute. Makes about 36–48 cookies.

7. For decorations, fill the cups of a muffin tin with things such as cereal flakes (great for fish scales), Cheerios, miniature chocolate pieces, and paint (food coloring and water to be brushed on with cotton swabs).

ACTIVITIES

UNDERWATER PAINTING

Help your child make an underwater painting. First, have her draw an underwater scene with crayons. Then "wash" it with blue tempera paint thinned with water to give it a realistic deep sea effect.

FISH BOWL WITHOUT WATER

Take glass jars (such as mustard or honey jars), shells, pebbles, bits of greenery, and pictures or stickers of fish. Have your child glue fish pictures (cut from magazines or drawn on colored paper) or stick fish stickers onto the outside of the glass jar. Then let her put shells, pebbles, and greenery inside the jar to finish the scene.

FISHING WITH MAGNETS

Make a fishing rod by tying a stick to one end of a piece of string and a magnet to the other. Cut several fish shapes 2" to 3" long. Clip a paper clip on each fish. With your child, put the fish into a bucket or other large container. Have your child see how many fish she can catch with her magnetic "hook."

GO FISH

Buy the card game "Go Fish," or make your own version. To make your own, simply cut out two fish of each color you wish to use and one odd-colored fish. Deal out the cards and draw to keep making pairs. The person left with the odd-colored fish loses.

Little Tommy Tucker

Little Tommy Tucker
Sings for his supper.

Is your house one filled with sounds? If you have a toddler, it surely is! Making sounds of all kinds is part of a toddler's very being. Animal sounds, people sounds, quiet sounds, loud sounds, melodic sounds, discordant sounds—toddlers love to make them all. As a child observes her environment and absorbs more of her surroundings, she experiments with her own capabilities to make sounds. Shrieking, squealing, whispering, and singing are language and sound experiments that fascinate a toddler. Banging, drumming, pounding, and tapping help polish motor skills. A toddler's day is filled with sounds from the first stretching yawn of the morning to the last sleepy sigh at night. Sometimes you might like the noise level to drop by several decibels, but try to relax and appreciate the noise as "sound" learning!

READINGS

Noisy by Shirley Hughes (Lothrop)
"Noisy noises!" begins this book that shows a day full of sounds in a household made up of toddler, baby, Mom, Dad, cat, and dog. The words are as delightful as the illustrations. Shirley Hughes has many fine books in this "Nursery Collection" that you may wish to look for.

Jungle Sounds by Colin and Jacqui Hawkins (Crown)
Farm Sounds by Colin and Jacqui Hawkins (Crown)
You're invited to snarl, snort, and roar along with the comically drawn jungle animals and moo, baa, and neigh along with the farm animals in these two enjoyable books.

Gobble Growl Grunt by Peter Spier (Doubleday)
Crash! Bang! Boom! by Peter Spier (Doubleday)
Page after page in these books is filled with sounds—that is, with words and pictures of the things that make the sounds. Both are now available with board pages.

RECITINGS

LISTEN!
(Sung to "Pop! Goes the Weasel")

All around my house I can hear,
Mounds of sounds—far and near.
All I do is listen real close and
SHHHH! They are there!

Do you think the sounds are still there,
If you're not there listening?
I'm not sure, but I think they still are,
SHHH! But I'm guessing!

GO ROUND AND ROUND THE HOUSE
(Sung to "Go Round and Round the Village")

Go round and round the house,
Go round and round the house,
Go round and round the house,
To see what you can hear.

Don't make a sound, just listen,
Don't make a sound, just listen,
Don't make a sound, just listen,
To hear what you can hear.

I hear the clock a-tickin',
I hear the clock a-tickin',
I hear the clock a-tickin',
That is one thing I hear.

Add others that you and your child may hear in your house.
I hear my kitten lickin', *etc.*
I hear the heater clickin', *etc.*
I hear the wind a-whistlin', *etc.*

RECIPES

The following two recipes involve "noisy" foods that children will love to listen to as they crunch.

POPCORN CHEWIES

Popcorn is fun to do as well as to eat. There are some popcorn activities below, too.

1. In a medium saucepan, stir together ½ cup peanut butter and 2 tablespoons honey. Beat in 2 eggs, stirring constantly over medium heat until the mixture boils and leaves the sides of the pan.

2. Remove from the heat and stir in 2 tablespoons margarine and 2 teaspoons vanilla.

3. Add 2 cups popped popcorn and ½ cup chopped peanuts and stir until thoroughly mixed.

4. Drop by rounded teaspoons onto waxed paper. Cool till firm.

BOWLING BALLS

Bowling is a noisy and exciting game. Try these bowling ball cookies.

1. In a medium mixing bowl, stir together 1 cup Grape Nuts cereal (or other crunchy nugget cereal), ½ cup finely crushed graham crackers, ½ cup finely snipped dried apricots, ½ cup finely chopped pecans, and ¼ cup sifted powdered sugar.

2. Stir in ¼ cup light corn syrup and 1 tablespoon orange juice. With buttered hands, shape into ¾ inch balls.

3. Roll the balls in ¼ cup cocoa powder. Store in a covered container. Makes about 36 cookies.

ACTIVITIES

POPCORN ACTIVITIES

■ Pretend to be popcorn by jumping up and down or hopping. Perhaps one time your child might like to be a kernel that refuses to pop.

123

■ Sing the following songs about popcorn:

POP, POP, POP, MY CORN
(Sung to "Row, Row, Row Your Boat")

Pop, pop, pop my corn,
Pop it big and white.
Popping, popping, popping, popping,
'til it is just right.

POPCORN IN A POT
(Sung to "I'm a Little Teapot")

I'm a little popcorn in a pot,
Heat me up and watch me pop.
When I get all fat and white, I'm done,
Popping corn is lots of fun.

BLOCK BOWLING

Set up some large cardboard blocks (or wooden ones if that's all you have available) in whatever pattern your child wishes. Roll a ball at them to knock them down. Start close to the blocks to assure some beginning success. Keeping score is not necessary.

LISTENING EXPERIMENTS

You can set up many listening experiments for your child. Have her listen to the "snap, crackle, pop" of rice cereal. Either make a tape of some familiar sounds around the house, or blindfold your child and then produce some sounds for her to identify. She may wish to make some sounds for you to identify, too.

Chapter Nine

SEPTEMBER

Colorful and Shapely Treasures

September is back-to-school time for older children. Your little one may have an older brother or sister or neighbor or friend who will be returning to school. As the students go off, you and your little one can "play school," exploring the concepts of color and shape (in this chapter) and the alphabet and counting (in the next chapter).

Please keep in mind that you shouldn't expect your child to "learn" these concepts in a final, down-pat way. Exposure to the ideas through books and play is all that is being suggested here.

So look around you and begin tuning into the vibrant colors and distinctive shapes you see. Get ready to explore these two treasures with your child.

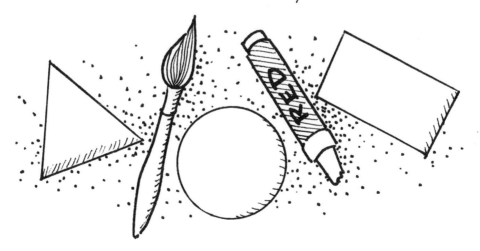

FIRST WEEK

One Thing At A Time

One thing at a time,
And that done well,
Is a very good rule,
As many can tell.

Would you rather spend a whole difficult year trying to toilet train your two year old or one smooth day guiding your three year old through a process she's ready for? Would you rather struggle for months trying to teach your two year old the alphabet or breeze through the ABCs for one playful day with an enthusiastic three year old? Everything will happen when the time is right. Children learn to walk, talk, eat with a fork, and ride a bike in their own time. He'll conquer each milestone eventually, so why rush it? It doesn't matter whether a child began to crawl at six months or eight months. The important thing is that he learned when he was ready. Given the time and the room to grow, children will reach the stars.

The next eight sections offer activities to introduce your little one to colors, shapes, numbers, and letters. Some children will be ready to grasp concepts that others won't. Don't panic if your toddler isn't ready yet. Don't push him—just expose him to a rich environment, wait for the signs of interest, and then watch him blossom. Like a seed planted in fertile soil, your child will flourish—in his own good time.

READINGS

Leo the Late Bloomer by Robert Kraus (Harper Junior Books)

Leo, a tiger cub, couldn't do anything right. His father was very concerned that Leo couldn't read, write, draw, speak, or eat neatly. But Leo's mother wasn't worried, and said Leo was just a late bloomer. Given time, Leo did bloom, to everyone's delight.

Max's First Word by Rosemary Wells (Dial Books for Young Readers)

Little bunny Max, much to his sister's dismay, could only say one word. All her prodding and coaxing couldn't make Max speak any sooner. But when he was finally ready, was he ever impressive!

Pig Pig Grows Up by David McPhail (E.P.Dutton)

Pig Pig refused to grow up—he just wasn't ready. Then one day he did, and he did it in style!

RECITINGS

IN MY OWN GOOD TIME
(Sung to "London Bridge")

Someday I'll be big and strong,
Big and strong, big and strong.
Someday I'll be big and strong,
In my own good time.

I won't need to nap all day,
Nap all day, nap all day.
I won't need to nap all day,
In my own good time.

I'll learn piano and sing along,
Sing along, sing along.
I'll learn piano and sing along,
In my own good time.

I'll read a book all right, not wrong,
Right, not wrong; right, not wrong.
I'll read a book all right, not wrong,
In my own good time.

SOON ENOUGH
(Sung to "She'll Be Coming Round the Mountain")

She'll be tying her own shoes soon enough,
She'll be tying her own shoes soon enough,
She'll be tying her own shoes,
She'll be tying her own shoes,
She'll be tying her own shoes soon enough.
Ya-hoo!

Add whatever else fits for your child.
She'll be saying her ABCs soon enough, *etc.*
She'll be writing her own name soon
    enough, *etc.*
She'll be going to the bathroom soon
    enough, *etc.*
She'll be sharing and helping out soon
    enough, *etc.*

RECIPES

HOMEMADE BREAD
The lesson to be learned here is that you can't rush baking bread. The yeast needs a certain amount of time to rise—so don't rush!

1. Mix together 2 cups warm water (test it on your wrist so it's not hot enough to kill the yeast), 1-½ tablespoons dry yeast, and 2 tablespoons honey. Stir to dissolve. Let sit for 5 minutes.

2. Add 1 tablespoon salt and 1 cup plain yogurt. Mix together thoroughly.

3. Stir in about 7-½ cups flour (whatever combination you choose: part white, whole wheat, etc.) Add enough that the dough starts to leave the sides of the bowl.

4. Knead for about 5–10 minutes, or until the dough feels smooth and satiny and springs back when you poke it with your finger.

5. Cut in half. Knead each half a little more. Shape into loaves. Put in greased loaf pans, cover with waxed paper and let rise in a warm spot for about 30 minutes.

6. Bake in preheated 350° oven for about 40 minutes.

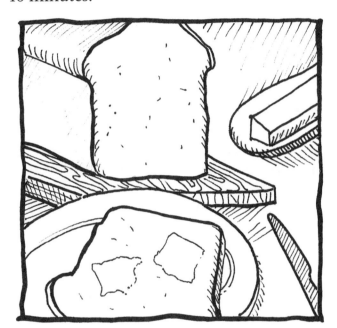

ORANGE GELATIN
The lesson to be learned here is that making gelatin can't be rushed. Gelatin needs time to set.

1. In a large bowl, mix 2 envelopes un-flavored Knox gelatin with ¼ cup sugar; add 1-½ cups orange juice, heated to boiling; stir until gelatin is completely dissolved.

2. With a wire whip or rotary beater, blend in 2 cups plain yogurt and reserved juice from one 11-ounce can of mandarin oranges. Chill until the mixture is the consistency of un-beaten egg whites.

3. Stir in mandarin oranges. Pour into an 11" x 7" pan and chill until firm.

ACTIVITIES

GLUING

Any gluing activity will help illustrate the point of allowing enough time for things to happen. If a gluing project is handled before it's completely dried, things can get messy.

Try this as a gluing project: Spread glue on a piece of dark-colored construction paper in whatever design you'd like. Give your child varied spices and have him sprinkle them onto the glue to make a picture that can be enjoyed by sniffing as well as looking.

PAINTING

A painting is another good example of something that shouldn't be rushed. Proper drying time is important.

Try this to illustrate the point: Spread a blob of paint on the top section of a piece of paper. Have your child hold the paper up while the paint is still very wet and runny. Watch what happens to the paint if the paper's moved before the paint's ready. Have her paint with the same paint, and this time give it a chance to dry. Help her notice the difference.

SIMPLE BALL GAMES

Play a simple ball game. Take turns pretending to be "ready" and not "ready." Have one person pitch the ball to the batter before the batter is ready or toss a ball to a partner before the partner is ready to catch it, to show some examples of not being ready. Then enjoy the games, pay attention to being ready, and have fun.

128

SECOND WEEK

Colors

Roses are red, lavender's blue,
If you will have me, I will have you.
Lilies are white, rosemary's green,
If you are king, I will be queen.

If you've ever wondered what's so special about color, give a box of crayons to a toddler and you'll have your answer. Color invites endless experimentation. Bold splashes of vivid colors and wispy touches of soft colors add brightness and excitement to empty spaces waiting to come to life. A child's eyes sparkle and his pride soars when he sees the beautiful colors he's made. At this age, a toddler's artwork isn't sophisticated or accurate. He probably doesn't know the names of the colors, but he certainly knows they're all waiting for him to use them. And that's all that matters right now. As you use various colors with your child, call them by their names, and eventually your child will be ready to remember and distinguish one from another. The important thing is to offer many colorful experiences to enrich your child's life and to widen his colorful world.

READINGS

There are so many fine books that introduce children to the world of color, you should have no difficulty finding good choices at your library. Be sure to look for bright, bold colors, vivid and true. You'll want to begin with the basic colors of blue, red, green and yellow, and then expand to other combinations.

Brown Bear, Brown Bear, What Do You See? by Bill Martin, Jr., illustrated by Eric Carle (Holt, Rinehart & Winston)

A great rhyme, repeating rhythm, and simple, bold illustrations combine to make this introductory color-concepts book a real winner.

Mouse Paint by Ellen Stoll Walsh (Harcourt Brace Jovanovich)

Three white mice explore the world of color as they experiment with three jars of paint—red, yellow, and blue. This is a spunky and enjoyable story.

The Bee: A Colorful Adventure of a Bee Who Left Home One Monday Morning and What He Found Along the Way by Lisa Campbell Ernst (Lothrop, Lee & Shepard)
The bold and bright illustrations and simple story make this a pleasant color book.

Other excellent color books include these:
Planting a Rainbow by Lois Ehlert (Harcourt Brace Jovanovich)
Color Zoo by Lois Ehlert (Harper Junior Books)
Eating the Alphabet: Fruits and Vegetables From A to Z by Lois Ehlert (Harcourt Brace Jovanovich)
Color Dance by Ann Jonas (Greenwillow)
Colors To Know by Karen Gundersheimer (Harper Junior Books)
Richard Scarry's Color Book by Richard Scarry (Random)
My Shirt is White by Dick Bruna (Price Stern)
John Burningham's Colors by John Burningham (Crown)
Colors by Shirley Hughes (Lothrop)
Busy Bear's Refrigerator by Harriet Margolin (Putnam Publishing Group)
Is it Red? Is it Yellow? Is it Blue? by Tana Hoban (Greenwillow)
Of Colors and Things by Tana Hoban (Greenwillow)

RECITINGS

COLORS EVERYWHERE

I look around my world and see
Colors everywhere.
Greens on plants and grass and trees,
And leaves up in the air.

Reds of apples, reds of berries,
Reds of roses, too.
Yellow flowers, yellow bees,
And sun to warm me through.

Sky-blue blue, ocean blue,
Blues so deep and true.
Purples and pinks, on flowers I think,
Are a colorful sight, too.

Clouds are white and black is night,
And brown is the ground at my feet.
I see colors everywhere
And think they are so neat!

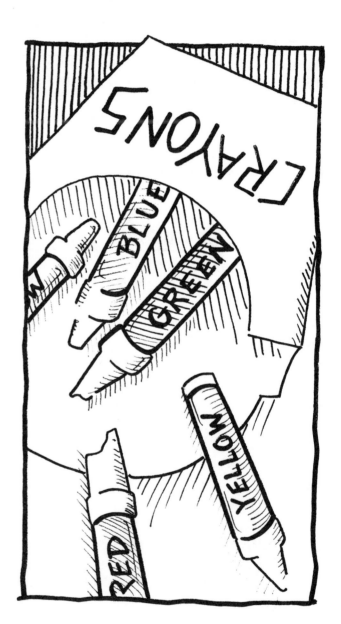

TEN LITTLE COLORS
(Sung to "Ten Little Indians")

One little, two little, three little colors,
Four little, five little, six little colors,
Seven little, eight little, nine little colors,
Ten colors in a row.

Red and blue and yellow—1, 2, 3,
Green and orange and purple—4, 5, 6,
Brown and white and black—7, 8, 9,
Just one more to go.

One more color to make all ten,
Which shall I choose? How will it end?
I think I'll pick pink. Can we sing it again?
I love my colors so!

RECIPES

RAINBOW FRUIT SALAD
Combine blue blueberries, red strawberries, green grapes, yellow bananas, purple grapes, orange oranges (and perhaps black raisins, brown nuts, and white coconut) in a clear bowl. You may wish to play a game with your child as you eat the salad together. Using colors she knows, ask her to eat one piece of a color. When she's followed that command, give her another. She may want to give you a command, too.

COLORFUL SALAD
Combine the following colorful vegetables to make a pretty and delicious salad.
> Green lettuce, broccoli, peppers, zucchini
> Purple cabbage
> Red tomatoes, peppers
> Yellow squash, peppers
> Orange carrots
> White cucumber, cooked potatoes

Mix them all up and serve with your favorite salad dressing. You may wish to add to or delete from the list. Talk about the colors with your child as you eat.

ACTIVITIES

I SPY
Choose something red that is clearly visible in the room where you and your child are and say, "I spy something red." Have the child guess what the object is by identifying it by color. If your child isn't sure what red is, show her something that matches the color you want her to find. Let her have a turn at being the person who "spies," too.

COLOR BOX
Fill a shoe box or other such box with objects of different colors. Have your child take one item out and tell you what color he thinks it is. If he only knows two colors, just put objects of those two colors in the box. Add more as he masters the new colors.

COLOR COLLAGE
Cut out objects of different shapes and colors and spread them out on the table. Have your child glue the different colors onto a piece of construction paper in any design she wishes. She may wish to add crayon designs, too. If she only wants to use her favorite color, that's fine. If she only wants to use the colors she knows how to say, fine. If she wants to use them all, fine. Anything goes. As she adds various objects, you can say things like, "Oh, I like that *orange* square," or "That's a nice *blue* kitty-cat," to reinforce the color names.

131

Colors—Part Two

Which came first, the chicken or the egg? Which comes first, an introduction to all the colors, or spending lots of time with one? No one knows the answer to the first question, and only you can answer the second. You know what will work best with your child. For some children, an initial look at the whole picture is a helpful introduction as it gives them a general overview of the subject. Others learn best one piece at a time, with each additional piece helping to broaden the foundation until the overview is reached.

The previous section offered general color ideas, exposing children to the many colors around them. This section will show you what to do with just one color at a time. You may wish to do this section's activities now and use the previous section's ideas as a review after your child knows several colors really well. You choose whatever is best for you. But whenever you feel your child is ready to play with a color, plan an entire day surrounded by one color. If your child's favorite color is red, have a red day where everything from breakfast to clothes to toys to lunch to books to songs to dinner to bath to bedtime is RED!

Brainstorm with your child and have a red-letter day with some color fun together.

READINGS

The Mystery of the Missing Red Mitten by Steven Kellogg (Dial Books for Young Readers; pb Dial Books for Young Readers)

Annie is enjoying herself playing in the snow until she realizes she has lost her red mitten. As she sets out to find it, the reader discovers many other hidden red objects. The illustrations are all in black and white except for the partially hidden red objects.

There are several other books that use a single color through the story in this series by Stephen Kellogg. ***The Mystery of the Flying Orange Pumpkin*** and ***The Mystery of the Stolen Blue Paint*** are two of them.

Clifford, the Big Red Dog by Norman Bridwell (Scholastic, Inc.)

This book is the first of many books about Clifford, the famous, lovable big red dog who belongs to Emily Elizabeth. Children love him, and they love the situations Clifford gets into because of his size. Look for some of the others: ***Clifford Gets a Job***, ***Clifford Takes a Trip***, ***Clifford and the Grouchy Neighbors***, ***Clifford's Christmas***, ***Clifford's Family***, ***Clifford's Kitten***, and ***Clifford's Riddles***.

My Red Umbrella by Robert Bright (Morrow)

A little girl and her red umbrella become a shelter for many animals during a sudden rainstorm.

Other red books include ***Big Red Barn*** by Margaret Wise Brown (Harper & Row) and ***Big Red Bus*** by Ethel and Leonard Kessler (Doubleday).

RECITINGS

SING A SONG OF COLORS
(Sung to "Sing a Song of Sixpence)

Sing a song of colors,
Of red and blue and green,
So many pretty colors
All around I've seen;
The yellow sun shines on me,
It makes the world look bright.
Without the many colors, it would
Always look like night!

Imagine everything black,
Or everything all blue,
Your face, your food, your house,
And your mom and daddy, too;
Blue pancakes, blue bananas,
Blue noses and blue toes,
I think the world would look silly,
If blue is what God chose.

COLORS
(Sung to "The Mulberry Bush")

Purple is made with red and blue,
Red and blue,
Red and blue.
Purple is made with red and blue,
Where is purple hiding?

Sing verses for other color blends, like these:
Orange is made with yellow and red, *etc.*
Green is made with yellow and blue, *etc.*
Brown is made with red, yellow and blue, *etc.*
Have your child look for objects of the color mentioned in the song.

RECIPES

Have fun making recipes and serving food that is the color of the day. Below are some suggestions for different colored foods.

PURPLE COW SHAKES

1. Pour a 6-ounce can of frozen grape juice concentrate and 1 cup milk into a blender.
2. Scoop in 2 cups vanilla ice cream.
3. Blend for 20 seconds.
4. Sip through straws.
You can make a "Green Cow" by blending pistachio ice cream with milk, a "Red Cow" by blending strawberry ice cream with milk, or a "Brown Cow" by blending chocolate ice cream with milk.

COLOR BLOX

Knox Blox are fun to make and eat because children can pick them up with their fingers. Make the color of the day and cut them into squares or cookie-cutter shapes. Use grape juice for purple, cranberry juice for red, limeade for green, orange juice for orange, and grapefruit juice or lemonade for yellow. To make Knox Blox:

1. Sprinkle 4 envelopes Knox unflavored gelatin over 1 cup cold fruit juice; let stand 1 minute.
2. Add 3 cups fruit juice heated to boiling, and stir until gelatin is completely dissolved.
3. Pour into a 13" x 9" baking pan. Chill until firm.
4. Cut into 1" squares or cut shapes with cookie cutters. Makes about 9 dozen squares.

ACTIVITIES

On your specific Color Day, try to do as much, eat as much, read as much, wear as much, and

133

play with as much of that one color as you can. Below are some projects you can do.

COLOR DAY FINGERPAINT

Make fingerpaint in the color of your Color Day.

1. Mix 2 cups flour and 2 teaspoons salt together.

2. Add 2-½ cups cold water. Beat until smooth.

3. Gradually add 2 cups hot water and boil until clear.

4. Beat until smooth. Add food coloring. Store in jars.

COLOR DAY PUPPETS

Make puppets of the color, either with felt that you cut out and glue or sew, or with paper bags your child can color with crayons or paint, or with socks of the right color. Have your child decorate the puppet as he wishes.

COLORS BOOK

Do one page for each color you work with. On each page, your child may wish to draw a line or a picture with a crayon of the color, glue a piece of material or yarn or paper of the color, or do anything else you think of with the color. Save each page, and when there are several, compile them into a book. Punch out holes and fasten the book together by tying rainbow ribbon or yarn through the holes.

FOURTH WEEK

Shapes

Ring around the rosy,
A pocketful of posies.
Ashes, ashes,
We all fall down.

If you put down this book right now and looked around, you could easily find the shapes of circles, squares, triangles, and rectangles all around you. There might be a rectangular picture on the wall, a circular clockface, a triangular bookend, a square tile. Keep looking, and you'll probably find dozens more. Everything is made up of shapes, of differing sizes and combinations of shapes. An ice cream cone is a triangle with a circle on top. Learning to recognize and identify shapes is truly child's play, because it's such fun. Spend some time with your toddler doing the things described below, and see what shapes up as you do!

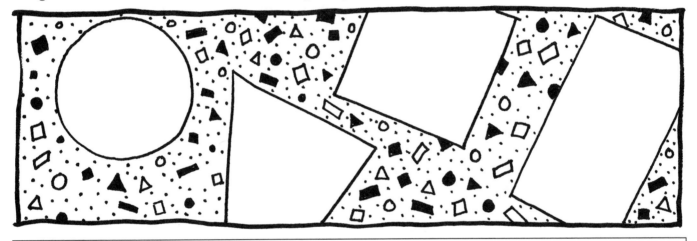

READINGS

Round and Round and Round by Tana Hoban (Greenwillow)

This is just one of the exceptional books by Tana Hoban in which she uses her photography to teach a concept. The reader is enticed to find all the round shapes naturally hidden in the everyday objects of the photographs. Also by this author are ***Shapes, Shapes, Shapes*** (Greenwillow), ***Circles, Triangles and Squares*** (Macmillan), and ***Dots, Spots, Speckles and Stripes*** (Greenwillow).

Busy Bear's Room: A Book About Shapes by Harriet Margolin (Grosset and Dunlop)

As Busy Bear tries to show the reader his room filled with shapes, his dog tries to catch his cat, making a simple and funny storyline for the book.

Look Around! by Leonard Everett Fisher (Viking Kestrel)

Circle, square, rectangle, and triangle are introduced to the young readers of this book in an enjoyable and colorful way.

RECITINGS

SHAPES
(Sung to "Frère Jacques")

Circles, squares,
Circles, squares,
Triangles,
Triangles.
Three of many shapes,
Three of many shapes,
In the world,
In the world.

Rectangles,
Rectangles,
Diamonds and spheres,
Diamonds and spheres.
Three more lovely shapes,
Three more lovely shapes,
In the world,
In the world.

As you sing this song with your child, make the shapes either with your hands and body or by having drawn them earlier and holding them up at the appropriate time in the song.

THE WHEELS OF A BUS ARE ROUND, ROUND, ROUND
(Sung to "The Wheels of the Bus")

The wheels of a bus are round, round, round,
Round, round, round,
Round, round, round.
The wheels of a bus are round, round, round.
Circles are round.

The windows of a bus are square, square, square,
Square, square, square,
Square, square, square.
The windows of a bus are square, square, square.
Windows are squares.

The keys of a bus are triangles,
Triangles, triangles.
The keys of a bus are triangles.
Keys are triangles.

The seats of a bus are rectangles,
Rectangles, rectangles.
The seats of a bus are rectangles.
Seats are rectangles.

RECIPES

Bake cut-out cookies using circular, square, triangular, and rectangular cookie cutters. Use your favorite recipe and let your toddler help roll out the dough and cut the dough with the cookie cutters.

APRICOT ROUNDS

1. Preheat oven to 375°. Grease cookie sheets.

2. In a large mixer bowl, beat ¼ cup margarine and ¾ cup packed brown sugar until mixture is well combined.

3. Add ½ cup vanilla yogurt and ½ teaspoon vanilla.

4. Add 1 cup quick-cooking rolled oats, ¾ cup flour, ¼ cup wheat germ, ½ teaspoon

baking soda, and ½ teaspoon cinnamon. Beat until well mixed.

5. Drop dough by rounded teaspoons about 2" apart onto greased cookie sheets. Press a piece of dried apricot in the top of each cookie (cut the apricots into quarters).

6. Bake for 10–12 minutes or until the cookies are golden. Let them cool 1 minute. With a pancake turner, lift cookies onto cooling rack to finish cooling. Makes about 36 cookies.

DIAMOND BARS

The trick to this treat is in the cutting. To get diamond shapes, cut six equal rows (5 cutting lines) even with the long sides of the pan. Then, cut slanting lines across the pan (at a 45° angle), keeping the lines as even as you can.

1. Preheat oven to 350°. Grease a 15" x 10" x 1" pan.

2. Mix 2 eggs, ½ cup brown sugar, and ⅔ cup cooking oil with a wooden spoon until well combined.

3. Add 1-¾ cups flour, 1 teaspoon baking powder, 1 teaspoon cinnamon, and ¼ teaspoon salt. Stir until well mixed.

4. Stir in 1 cup shredded carrots (2–3 medium carrots) and ¾ cup raisins. Pour into greased baking pan and spread evenly.

5. Bake for 22–25 minutes or until toothpick comes out clean. Let cool in pan.

6. When cool, spread with **CREAM CHEESE FROSTING:** Beat together one 3-ounce package cream cheese, 2 tablespoons margarine, and 1 teaspoon vanilla until light and fluffy. Gradually beat in 2 cups sifted powdered sugar.

7. Cut into diamonds. Makes 42 bars.

Without baking anything special, you probably have a kitchen full of food shapes that you can share with your toddler. Try some of the following: *circles*—cookies, pancakes, oranges, plums, peaches, English muffins, biscuits; *squares*—crackers, sandwiches, pieces of cake; *triangles*—pieces of pie, wedges of cheese; and *rectangles*—ice cream bars, slices from tall loaves of bread, some cookies, sheet cakes, etc.

ACTIVITIES

SHAPE COLLAGES

Cut paper, cardboard, or even scrap pieces of wood into various shapes and let your child glue himself a wonderful collage that he can decorate.

SHAPE I SPY

Play the "I Spy" game using shapes. You might spy something "shaped like a circle." Let your child guess. Take turns.

SHAPE SEARCH

Make some very simple and obvious hidden-shape pictures for your child to find the shapes and color them in. Once she gets good at spying the hidden shapes, make it a bit more difficult.

PLAY CLAY

Clay is a wonderful medium for toddlers to manipulate and experiment with. Circles are certainly the easiest shape to make (just roll a ball and flatten it), but you can show your child how to form some of the other shapes.

Here is a recipe for play clay, should you wish to make your own: Cook together over medium heat 2 cups flour, 1 cup salt, 2 cups water, 4 teaspoons cream of tartar, and food coloring until the mixture comes away from the pan. Cool until you can knead out lumps without burning your hands. Cool even further for your child to handle. Store in a tightly covered bowl.

Chapter Ten

OCTOBER

Treasures As Easy As 1, 2, 3 and A, B, C

*More school-play activities abound in this chapter.
There are countless books available on counting and even more
about the alphabet. In addition to the many books referenced, there are
lots of songs, recipes, and activities suggested in this chapter. You'll have
no difficulty finding ways to explore the treasures of counting and the
treasures of the alphabet. Choose some of your favorites
and have a good time with your little one.*

FIRST WEEK

Counting

One for the money,
Two for the show,
Three to get ready,
And four to go!

Most children know the concept "two" very well. When offered a cookie, they want two because they have two hands! When learning about their own bodies, "two" keeps coming up—two eyes, two ears, two arms, two hands, two legs, two feet. By the time a child is two years old, he's ever so proud to hold up two fingers and tell everyone how old he is.

This is a good way to teach beginning number concepts to your little one. Learning numbers from his body and his immediate surroundings gives more meaning and depth to the subject than any other method because it links them directly to the child. How many people are in his family? How many fingers are on his hand? How many books are on his shelf?

Number concepts should be learned very generally at first. Number games, rhymes and songs, and books which introduce number concepts give a toddler a beginning feeling of comfort with numbers. This section deals with general number concepts for those of you who wish to begin a casual relationship between your child and numbers. The next section will deal with counting and the actual numbers themselves.

READINGS

There are many books that use numbers casually throughout the storyline of the book. Reading such a book is a great introduction to numbers. Look for some of these:

One Step, Two... by Charlotte Zolotow (Lothrop)

A little girl and her mother go for a walk and count things on the way. During the leisurely walk, the little girl points out many things her mom would've missed in her haste.

Over in the Meadow by Olive Wadsworth, illustrated by Ezra Jack Keats (Scholastic, Inc.)

This is a gentle counting book incorporating the numbers one through ten as the reader counts the many wonderful creatures in the meadow. Its pictures and words are equally beautiful.

Ten, Nine, Eight by Molly Bang (Greenwillow)

This soft, soothing rhyme is a wonderful counting book as well as a bedtime book.

Also good are **Ten in a Bed** by Mary Rees (Little), **Harriet Goes to the Circus: A Number Concept Book** by Betsy Maestro (pb Crown), and **Busy Bear's Closet** by Harriet Margolin (Grosset & Dunlap).

RECITINGS

THIS OLD MAN

(Hannah West), she played one,
She played knick-knack on her thumb.
With a knick-knack, paddy-whack, give a
     dog a bone,
(Hannah West) came rolling home.

140

(Hannah West), she played two,
She played knick-knack on her shoe, *etc.*

(Hannah West), she played three,
She played knick-knack on my knee, *etc.*

four—floor
five—hive
six—sticks
seven—heaven
eight—gate
nine—spine
ten—over again!

Use your fingers to indicate the numbers as you sing this song with your children.

A SILLY STORY

I have a silly story,
I know it really well.
Listen very closely,
And my story I will tell.

There was a girl named Tilly,
Who looked a little silly.
Her hair was blue,
Her noses—two,
And her four arms were always chilly.

She walked a little different,
Than most people we know.
With five big feet,
It was real neat,
To watch her come and go.

I know this all sounds silly,
I know it sounds untrue.
You might be right,
But what a sight,
If I'm right and not you!

| RECIPES | ACTIVITIES |

RECIPES

HUNGRY CATERPILLAR FRUIT SALAD

In **The Hungry Caterpillar** (*see reference in the May chapter*), the caterpillar eats holes through many foods. You can follow the same idea as you make a fruit salad with your child.

1. You will need 1 apple, 1 pear, 1 plum, 4 strawberries, and 1 orange. Cut each fruit except the strawberries into bite-size pieces.

2. Have the fruit available as you recite the following: "On Monday, he ate through one apple—but he was still hungry." Have your child put in a bowl one piece of apple.

3. Then continue: "On Tuesday, he ate through two pears, but he was still hungry. Put two pieces of pear into the bowl." "On Wednesday, he ate through three plums, but he was still hungry..." "On Thursday, he ate through four strawberries, but he was still hungry..." "On Friday, he ate through five oranges, but he was still hungry..."

4. Mix up the fruit pieces your child has put in his bowl, and then add more of whatever he'd like. You may, of course, substitute any fruits.

COUNTING FRUIT KABOBS

1. Cut up 1 banana, 1 apple, 1 melon, and 1 pear (or any other combination you'd like).

2. Get skewers, and as you put each piece of fruit on the skewer, count.

3. Dip the kabobs in orange juice, roll in coconut, and eat!

Food lends itself to number play. Count cookies as you put them on the cookie sheet to be baked; count salad ingredients as you toss them in the salad bowl; count raisins and nuts as you make a snack mix.

ACTIVITIES

COUNTING WALK

Go for a leisurely walk with your child when you can truly take your time. Let your child point out things of interest to him and you can point out what interests you, too. Count the number of squirrels, or brightly colored trees, or mailboxes you see along the way.

CATEGORIES

On a rainy day or a day when you're looking for something to do together, sort some of your child's toys by putting them into category piles. All the trucks might go in one pile, the books in another, the building blocks in another. First analyze which pile is bigger. Then count. Have fun with numbers.

TOWER COUNTING

Every toddler loves to build towers and loves even more to knock them down. This time, as you build, count to see how many blocks you can get in the tower before it either falls or gets knocked down.

There are many ways for you and your child to have fun with numbers. As you do your daily chores and go through your daily routines, keep numbers in mind, and you'll find many opportunities to bring them into the conversation through songs, games, and rhymes.

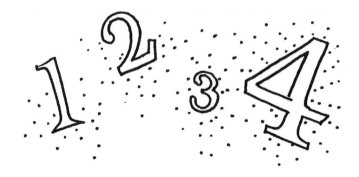

SECOND WEEK

Counting—Part Two

How many opportunities do you take each day to count to—and with—your child? Perhaps you count as you help your toddler dress in the morning. ("One, two, buckle my shoe.") Maybe you count as part of a game or song you are sharing. ("One little, two little, three little Indians.") Or perhaps you count in hopeful pursuit of maintaining your patience while waiting for your little one to complete a task. ("By the time I count to ten, please have your toys picked up!") All these counting opportunities are excellent ways to familiarize your child with counting, numbers, and some of their uses.

When you see flowers, stop and count them with your child. Count slowly and give him ample time to repeat each number after you say it. When coloring with your child, point to each crayon and count them slowly, having your child count, too. When your little one helps set the table, have her count out the number of forks and spoons she will need for each member of the family.

Provide as many counting opportunities as you naturally can during the course of each day, and your child will get familiar and comfortable with numbers. Read this section's activities for further ideas.

READINGS

Counting Wildflowers by Bruce McMillan (Lothrop)

With beautiful photographs of real wildflowers and colored-in dots corresponding to each picture, Bruce McMillan has produced a wonderful counting book.

Ten Black Dots by Donald Crews (Greenwillow)

What can one do with ten black dots? Donald Crews has produced a very clever counting book with them.

1, 2, 3 to the Zoo by Eric Carle (pb Philomel Books)

Readers will have fun counting all the zoo animals that are loaded on a colorful train.

Also look for ***Night Counting*** by Ann Morris (Harper Junior Books), ***I Can Count*** by Dick Bruna (Price Stern Sloan), ***Up to 10 and Down Again*** by Lisa Campbell Ernst (Lothrop), ***Count and See*** and ***1, 2, 3*** and ***Twenty-Six Letters and Ninety-Nine Cents*** all by Tana Hoban (Greenwillow), ***Numbers of Things*** by Helen Oxenbury (Delacorte), and ***Richard Scarry's Best Counting Book Ever*** by Richard Scarry (Random).

RECITINGS

TEN LITTLE INDIANS

One little, two little, three little Indians.
Four little, five little, six little Indians.
Seven little, eight little, nine little Indians.
Ten little Indian boys. *(Or "girls.")*

Then do it in reverse. You may also wish to substitute other words for "Indians", such as "fingers," "flowers," "cars," or "dishes."

I'VE GOT SOME PEANUTS IN MY HAND
(Sung to "He's Got the Whole World in His Hands")

I've got some peanuts in my hand,

I've got some yummy crunchy peanuts in
   my hand,
I've got some peanuts in my hand,
I've got some peanuts in my hand.

Can you count them—can you, can?
Can you count them—can you, can?
Can you count them—can you, can?
Can you count peanuts in my hand?

*You can change the number of peanuts or the ob-
jects in your hand and continue with your
song/game.*

RECIPES

NUTTY NUMBERS

1. Mix ½ cup margarine, 1 cup flour, ¼
cup honey, and 1 cup wheat germ in a bowl.
Mix well.

2. Take a small amount of the dough and
shape it into numbers by rolling "snakes" and
then shaping them.

3. Cover with chopped nuts. Gently press
the nuts into the dough.

4. Bake on a greased cookie sheet for 10
minutes at 350°.

NUMBER SANDWICHES

1. Make any of your favorite sandwiches—
egg salad, peanut butter, tuna fish, or toasted
cheese would be fine.

2. With a knife or a number-shaped cookie
cutter, cut the desired number out of the bread.
Make it as large as you can to use as much of

the sandwich as possible. Try to make as few
cuts as possible so you can serve the "frame"
the number was cut from, too. If you wish, use
a large paper number as a guide; lay it right on
top of the bread and cut around it.

3. You might like to have a different number each day, or let your child choose the
number she likes each day.

ACTIVITIES

NUMBER COLLAGE

Go through old magazines, cards,
catalogs, and calendars and look for numbers.
Choose one particular number or let your child
find any number she wants. Cut out all that
you wish. Then glue them onto a piece of
construction paper to make a number collage.

NUMBER SETS

Cut a very large number out of oaktag.
Then, draw right on the oaktag number sets of
objects appropriate to it. For example, if the
number is "2," draw two bunnies, two hats,
two doggies, two buttons, and two ice cream
cones. Have your child color them in and feel
the concept of "2."

NUMBER MATCHING GAME

Make up an easy matching game to play
with your child. Take index cards and write a
large number on each. For each number, draw
on a corresponding card a set of objects that
depicts that number. Mix the cards up and
have your child match the number cards to the
sets of picture cards.

NUMBER SIMON SAYS

Play a "Simon Says" game in which your
child has to follow verbal commands dealing
with numbers, such as "hold up two fingers"
or "jump up and down three times."

THIRD WEEK

ABC

Great A, little a,
Bouncing B,
The cat's in the cupboard,
And can't see me.

When should a child have the alphabet mastered? By the age of two and a half? Three? Three and a half? Should it be taught in nursery school? Should a child be considered ready for kindergarten if he doesn't know his alphabet cold? Should it be taught by letter names or letter sounds? There seem to be as many opinions on these questions as there are letters in the alphabet!

Whether you are of the opinion that early mastery gives a child a certain edge and confidence or of the opinion that a child will learn best and most expediently when he is truly ready, alphabet play works beautifully, for it casually exposes the child to the alphabet in a playful way so that when he is truly ready (whether at two or six), the foundation is there.

This section presents a list of ABC books, several recitings, and food and play ideas for the letters A through H. The following two sections will offer food and play activities for the letters I–Q and R–Z respectively.

There is much you can do to have fun with the alphabet. For example, you can declare Monday an A–Day and brainstorm to see how many "A" things you can see, do, eat, make, and say. Here are one food suggestion and one activity for each letter to get your creative minds in gear. Once you begin, you'll see how much fun your ABCs can be!

READINGS

There are literally hundreds of alphabet books in print. There are ABC books about cars, cats, animals; there are nonsense ABC books and ABC books with well-plotted stories; there are ABC books with simple illustrations and others with photographs. Below is a list of a few of the recommended books for you to choose from.

Anno's Alphabet by Mitsumasa Anno (Harper Junior Books; pb Harper Junior Books)

B is for Bear: An ABC by Dick Bruna (Price Stern)

John Burningham's ABC by John Burningham (Crown)

We Read: A to Z by Donald Crews (Greenwillow)

The Most Amazing Hide-and-Seek Alphabet Book by Robert Crowther (Viking Press)

ABC Bunny by Wanda Gag (Putnam Publishers; pb Putnam Publishers)

A Apple Pie by Kate Greenaway (Warne)

Teddybears ABC by Susanna Gretz (Macmillan)

ABC Say With Me by Karen Gundersheimer (Harper Junior Books)

A B See! by Tana Hoban (Greenwillow)

Twenty-Six Letters and Ninety-Nine Cents by Tana Hoban (Greenwillow)

I Unpacked My Grandmother's Trunk by Susan Ramsay Hoguet (Dutton)

Lucy and Tom's ABC by Shirley Hughes (Penguin USA; pb Penguin)

Helen Oxenbury's ABC of Things by Helen Oxenbury (pb Delacorte)

Curious George Learns the Alphabet by H. A. Rey (pb Houghton Mifflin)

Albert B. Cub and Zebra by Anne Rockwell (Harper Junior Books; Harper Junior Books)

Richard Scarry's ABC Word Book by Richard Scarry (Random)

Alligators All Around by Maurice Sendak (Harper Junior Books)

Dr. Seuss's ABC by Dr. Seuss (Beginner)

Hooper Humperdink...? Not Him! by Dr. Seuss (Beginner)

All in the Woodland Early: An ABC Book by Jane Yolen (Putnam Publishers; pb Putnam Publishers)

RECITINGS

ABC SONG
(Sung to "Twinkle, Twinkle Little Star")

A, B, C, D, E, F, G,
H, I, J, K, L, M, N, O, P,
Q, R, S and T, U, V,
W, X, and Y, and Z.
Now I know my ABCs,
Next time, won't you sing with me.

A IS AN APPLE
(Sung to "Twinkle, Twinkle Little Star")

A is an apple, big and red,
B is a ball to bounce on your head,
C is a cat, D's for my dad,
E is an elephant gray and glad,
F is for fish, and G is for green,
H is my house so nice and clean.
A through H, I know so well,
What comes next—I cannot tell!

A–H RECIPES and ACTIVITIES

 **Apple**

Apple Rings: Core and slice apples in ⅛" slices. Spread on a cookie sheet covered with plastic wrap. Dry in oven on lowest heat setting for 6–9 hours. Store in air-tight container.

Apple Star: Cut an apple in half—not at the stem, but crosswise through the middle—to see the star.

 **Ball**

Ball Cookies: Mix peanut butter, wheat germ, and dry milk powder to a consistency that allows you to form the mixture into balls. Refrigerate.

Ball Play: Play any kind of ball. Children at this age especially enjoy kicking and throwing balls like soccer balls or beachballs.

**Cat**

Cat Cereal: Pour your child's favorite cereal in a bowl, and in another bowl, pour milk. Have your child enjoy eating like a "kitty"!

Cat Collage: As there are so many ads in magazines with cats in them, cut some out and have your child glue together a cat collage.

**Daddy**

Daddy's Favorite: Bake Daddy's favorite cookie recipe in honor of him. At our house, Daddy's favorite is Tollhouse Cookies.

Daddy Specials: Plan a special "I Love Daddy" day for some time other than the traditional Father's Day and do things Daddy wants to do.

**Elephant**

Elephant Peanut Butter: Since elephants love peanuts, make your own peanut butter for E–Day. Simply put some roasted peanuts in your blender or food processor and blend. This is the best and healthiest peanut butter you'll ever taste.

Elephant Peanut Hunt: Buy a bag of peanuts in their shells, hide them around the house, and let your child have a peanut treasure hunt.

**Fish**

Fishy Crackers: Arrange Pepperidge Farm goldfish crackers on a large paper plate in the shape of a big fish for a "fishy" treat.

Fish Game: Cut out several fish-shaped cards. Have your child hold one at a time over a "pond" (a basket). Have her try to drop each fish back in the "pond."

**Green**

Greenest Salad: Use only green ingredients; include several kinds of lettuce, peppers, celery, cucumbers, broccoli, zucchini, etc.

Green Light: Play Red Light–Green Light using large cut-out red and green circles. Hold up the green circle when your child can "go" and the red circle when he should "stop."

**House**

House Crackers: Use graham crackers to build a two- or three-dimensional house. If you wish to "glue" pieces together in three dimensions, use frosting or peanut butter.

House Map: Draw together a very simple map of your house. Perhaps you can draw the outline and your child can fill in some of the room's furnishings.

FOURTH WEEK

Alphabet Play—Part Two

Keep playing with the alphabet. Here are ideas for letters I through Q.

RECITINGS

I IS FOR ICE CREAM
(Sung to "Twinkle Twinkle Little Star")

I is for ice cream, cool and sweet,
J is for jelly, what a treat,
K is kids, I'm proud to be,
L is lemons, so tart to me,

M's my mom, I love her so,
N's for numbers that I know,
O is orange, P—pumpkins round,
Q is my quilt I wrap around.
I through Q—I'm having fun,
The ABCs are two-thirds done!

I-Q RECIPES and ACTIVITIES

 **Ice Cream**

Ice Cream Balls: Use a melon baller to scoop balls of ice cream; arrange them on a plate as your own dessert art.

Science Experiment: Take several balls of ice cream. Put one on the kitchen counter, one in the refrigerator, and one in the freezer. Discuss what happens.

 **Jelly**

Jelly Roll Sandwich: Spread one slice bread with favorite jelly. Roll up jellyroll-style.

Jelly Jar Music: Save variously sized jelly jars. When you have three or more, fill each with varying amounts of water. Tap with a spoon to hear changes in pitch.

Kids

Kids Energy Mix: Mix together equal amounts of peanuts, raisins, other nuts, seeds, other dried fruit for a quick energy-boost snack.

Kids Collage: Have extra photos of your kids just lying around the house? Let your kids cut them up into a collage featuring themselves. If you don't have any old photos, use magazine pictures.

Lemon

Lemonade: Experiment with what it takes to get lemons to taste sweet enough to drink. Squeeze 2–3 lemons, add water, then add sugar, tasting all the way until it's right.

Taste Test: Discuss the different types of tastebuds. Let your child taste lemons for sour, baker's chocolate for bitter, sugar for sweet, and salt for salty (or other foods that represent each taste sensation).

Mommy

Mommy's Meal: Make a meal for Mom. Make it an easy one—perhaps her favorite sandwich for lunch. Choose something easy enough for the toddler to do himself.

Mommy Flowers: As far as we know, all Mommies love flowers. Have your child either pick some wild flowers out in the yard or make some simple paper ones to give to her.

Numbers

Number Cookies: Make your favorite recipe for cut-out cookies. Use number cookie-cutters to cut them out or roll the dough into long thin snakes and shape them into numbers.

Numbers Game: Play a simplified Simon Says game, giving commands such as "Simon says jump up and down two times" or "take three steps forward."

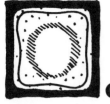

Orange

Orange Smiles: Cut oranges into quarters to eat with your child. Let him put the orange skin in his mouth to cover his teeth and have him look in a hand mirror to see his smile.

Orange Mix: Experiment with colors. Mix some primary colors together to get new ones. Red and yellow will make orange.

Pumpkin

Pumpkin Pizzas: Toast English muffins, spread on some spaghetti sauce and grated cheese, then top with jack-o-lantern-shaped eyes, nose, and mouth cut from vegetables.

Paper Pumpkins: Cut out many orange paper circles. Let your child decorate them like jack-o-lanterns. (You could also carve or decorate real pumpkins, which should be everywhere this time of the year.)

Quilt

Quilt Sandwich: Spread a piece of bread with peanut butter. Mark it off into squares by pressing a knife blade into the peanut butter. Give your child nuts, dried fruits, jellies, etc., to "sew" into the "quilt" to make a patchwork sandwich.

Quilt on Paper: Divide a piece of paper into equal sections. Have your child color them or decorate them however she wishes. It could be more a gluing activity than coloring if you choose.

Alphabet Play—Part Three

Build on the activities in the two previous sections with these ideas for the letters R through Z.

RECITINGS

R IS FOR RABBITS
(Sung to "Twinkle, Twinkle Little Star")

R is for rabbits cute and white,
S is the sun so strong and bright,
T is a shape I know real well
(Triangle is so hard to spell),
U an umbrella to keep me dry,

V my vegetables, fresh or fried,
W is wagon, X xylophone
With pretty sounds to play at home,
Y is yellow, bright and true,
Z is for the animal zoo.
That's my alphabet, A through Z,
I feel very PROUD of me!

I–R RECIPES and ACTIVITIES

 **Rabbit**

Rabbit Salad: Make a salad that a bunny would love. Have your child help you choose which garden treats your salad should include.

Rabbit Indoor Garden: Cut off a carrot top. "Plant" it in a shallow dish of water. Plant lettuce seeds in dirt to grow indoors. Watch for signs of growth.

 **Sun**

Sunrise Juice: Pour apricot nectar into glass. Tilt glass and slowly add cranberry juice. Watch the sunrise!

Sun-Shadows: If you can't go outside, use a flashlight as the "sun." Have your child step into the "sunlight" to find her shadow. Experiment with shadow sizes and shapes.

 **Triangle**

Tortilla Triangles: Cut 1 tortilla into 6 wedges, like a pie. Spread with mustard, sprinkle with ¼ cup grated cheese. Roll up, large end first, and secure with toothpick. Bake at 350° for 5 minutes. Let cool before eating.

Triangle Collage: Cut many different sized triangles out of colored construction paper. Glue onto a sheet of paper to make a geometric collage.

 **Umbrella**

Umbrella Shake: Mix in blender 1 cup milk, 2 cups strawberry yogurt, and one 10-ounce package frozen strawberries (thawed). Serve in tall glasses with a straw. Insert small umbrella in straw.

Umbrella Walk: Go for a rainy-day walk. Dress warmly; carry an umbrella; listen to the sounds of the rain on the umbrella.

 **Vegetables**

Vegetable People: Using toothpicks and chunks of vegetables (carrots, celery, potatoes, etc.), put together people.

Vegetable Guessing Game: Have a vegetable in mind, such as a cucumber. Give your child clues, one at a time, until she guesses it.

 **Wagon**

Wagons: Fill celery sections with peanut butter. Use toothpicks to attach carrot-slice wheels and a carrot-stick handle to make an edible wagon. Help your child remove the toothpicks when it's time to eat.

Wagon Ride: Treat your child to a ride in a real wagon if you have one or in a pretend wagon made of a big box or an old laundry basket. Attach a length of rope to pull the "wagon."

 **Xylophone**

Xylophone Snack: Place two strands of spaghetti 1" apart on a plate. Lay rectangular slices of cheese on top of and perpendicular to the spaghetti.

Xylophone Model: Take ten clean popsicle sticks. Lay two parallel to each other about 2" apart. Lay the other eight on top of the first two and perpendicular to them. Glue them all in place. Have your child color them if he wishes.

 **Yellow**

Yellow Fruit Candle: Lay a pineapple ring on plate. Put a tall, straight banana chunk in the hole of the pineapple slice. Eat your yellow candle.

Yellow Game: Play the "I'm Thinking Of" game with yellow things. Choose something in the room that's yellow, but only give one clue. Have your child guess what it is, and if she can't, give another clue. Take turns choosing yellow objects if your child's ready.

 **Zoo**

Zoo Animal Crackers: Grind ½ cup oatmeal in blender until fine. Add 2 teaspoons honey, ¼ teaspoon salt, ¾ cup flour, ¼ teaspoon soda. Cut in ¼ cup butter. Add 4 tablespoons buttermilk. Roll very thin. Cut with animal cookie cutters. Bake at 400° 10–12 min. on an ungreased cookie sheet.

Zoo Play: Role play various zoo animals. Add simple costumes if you wish. You could use facepaints and/or make-up, too.

Chapter Eleven

NOVEMBER

Treasures For Which We Are Thankful

November in America means Thanksgiving—a perfect holiday to share with your little one. Tell him about the first Thanksgiving, and then make it personally meaningful for him by thinking about all the things your family has to be thankful for.

One thing some people aren't particularly thankful for is winter, but you can brainstorm with your child and come up with many good things about winter. You might think about the Pilgrims' early life in America. We have more to help us than the Pilgrims did. Share this concept with your little one and try to help him see scary and sad situations in a more positive light. You have so many treasures for which to be thankful— most especially, for each other.

FIRST WEEK

Lengthening Days

As the days grow shorter,
The storms grow stronger.

If you were to count all the things you like about winter, could you do it on one hand? If you were to ask your child to count all the things she likes about winter, would she need two hands? Winter is rapidly approaching, and most likely, your children couldn't be happier! Children don't see snow and ice as potentially dangerous; they see them as definitely entertaining. Children don't feel the cold weather as raw and bitter; they feel it as invigorating. As much as you may dread the oncoming season, muster up some enthusiasm and spend special time with your child preparing for winter's joys.

READINGS

Animals in Winter by Vanessa Luff (Adam & Charles Black)

All animals need to prepare for the cold winter months, and this book explains how they do it.

The Winter Bear by Ruth Craft and Erik Blegvad (Atheneum)

While three children frolic and play during a cold winter day's walk, they discover a special treat stuck in the top of a hedge. We share their excitement through this beautifully illustrated rhyming book.

Winter Days by Harold Roth (Putnam Publishing Group)

This board book is one of real photographs of children enjoying winter with sledding, walking on ice, and warming up by the fire.

Two other good books are ***Snow*** by P. D. Eastman (Collins) and ***Winter's Coming*** by Eve Bunting (Harcourt Brace Jovanovich).

RECITINGS

WINTER'S COMING
(Sung to "Frère Jacques")

Winter's coming, winter's coming,
Animals scurry, animals scurry.
Gather nuts and seeds,
Enough for winter feed,
They must hurry, they must hurry.

Winter's coming, winter's coming,
Let's keep warm, let's keep warm.
More layers of clothes,
From our heads down to our toes,
We won't mind the storm, won't mind the storm.

Winter's coming, winter's coming,
I can't wait, I can't wait.
Sledding down the hills,
Frosty windowsills,
Winter's great, winter's great!

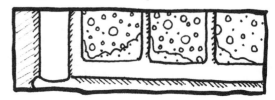

JACK AND JILL
(Sung to "Jack and Jill")

Jack and Jill went up a hill,
Pulling up their sleds;
Jack went fast, and Jill sped past,
But then she bumped her head.

Jack rushed over to see his sister,
And asked, "Are you OK?"
She just smiled for a long while,
Then said, "Let's go and play!"

RECIPES

INSTANT HOT CHOCOLATE
This recipe for hot chocolate mix that you make yourself has the advantage of your control over how much cocoa and sugar are used. Sift three times and store the mixture in the refrigerator.

1. Mix 1 cup dry milk powder, 2 tablespoons cocoa, and 1 tablespoon (or less) sugar.

2. To prepare hot chocolate, place 3–4 heaping teaspoons of the mixture in a cup. Stir in hot milk or hot water. Add a few drops of vanilla.

POPCORN
A fun thing to do on a cold winter day is pop popcorn. The warmth and aroma are almost as good as the taste itself. There are many ways to make popcorn, in a microwave or a special popcorn popper or a wok. Use the method you prefer, and then try some of these ideas.

■ Mix popped corn with peanuts, chocolate chips, raisins, sunflower seeds, and other dried fruits and/or nuts you like.

■ Make cheese popcorn by melting ¼ cup butter, then adding ⅓ cup grated cheddar or Parmesan cheese and 3 cups popped popcorn.

CARAMEL CORN
1. Mix ½ cup brown sugar, 6 tablespoons butter or margarine, 3 tablespoons light corn syrup, and ⅛ teaspoon salt in a 1-½ quart saucepan. Cook until butter melts and everything is mixed. Continue to cook until mixture begins to boil. Cook for 5 minutes without stirring.

2. Take pan off the burner. Stir in ¼ teaspoon baking soda and ¼ teaspoon vanilla.

3. Pour mixture over 8 cups popped popcorn in a 17" x 12" x 2" baking pan. Stir until all the popcorn is coated.

4. Bake in 300° oven for 15 minutes. Stir popcorn well with a wooden spoon and return to oven to cook for another 5–10 minutes.

5. Use a pancake turner to remove caramel corn from pan to a large bowl. Cool.

ACTIVITIES

ANIMAL ROLE PLAY
Children love animals and enjoy pretending to be them. After learning about how various animals prepare for winter, role play with your child some of the different things animals do. For example, you may wish to hide some shelled nuts around the house and have a squirrel nut hunt.

POPSICLE SLEDS

Sleds are a great toy. Although there may not be enough snow for a real sled to fly on, you can make simple sleds to play with indoors. Take six Popsicle sticks and glue four of them together side-by-side for the sled bed. Then glue the last two edge-on underneath the two outermost sticks to make the runners. Glue a large paper clip over the top of the four sticks to act as a steering bar. Allow plenty of time for the glue to dry. Then let your child decorate as desired with paint, crayons, or magic markers. (You may want to color the sticks first.) When the sleds are finished, make some hills for them to slide down on. You could use a book propped on a slant or a fat pillow covered with waxed paper.

WINTERTIME DRESSING HELPS

Wintertime dressing can be cumbersome and time-consuming with little ones.

■ You can make it into a game, perhaps by singing "Zip-A-Dee-Doo-Dah" (from Walt Disney's *Song of the South*) as you zip up jackets.

■ Or you can teach your little one how to put on his coat by himself. Lay his coat open on the floor, and have him stand facing it, hood or collar touching his toes, zipper side facing up. Have him bend down, put his arms into the sleeves, and then straighten up while swinging his arms with the coat on them over his head. (You can hold the coat tail to help with the "swinging" part.)

■ Practice putting on hats and mittens, using a doll.

■ Have a special place that she can reach where your child can always leave her mittens and hat, a boot tray for boots, and a hook for her jacket so she can feel proud of herself as she learns to help put things in their right places.

SECOND WEEK

Pop! Goes the Weasel

All around the cobbler's bench
The monkey chased the weasel,
The monkey thought t'was all in fun,
Pop! Goes the weasel.

What makes "Pop! Goes the Weasel" such a well-loved nursery rhyme? The same intrigue that's present in the games of Peek-a-boo and Hide and Seek: the element of surprise! The anticipation of the surprise when the jack-in-the-box springs up is so keen that a child will sit and crank the handle and squeal with delight every time it happens. It's the same anticipation that lends excitement to each succeeding Peek-a-boo game. How will Mommy surprise me this time? And with Hide and Seek, where can I hide this time to really surprise everyone?

This fascination can ease you through many otherwise difficult situations. Peek-a-boo between baby and parent begins to teach the concept of "Daddy goes away, but Daddy always comes back." A quick game of Peek-a-boo can distract a determined two year old, making your goals easier to obtain. A high-spirited game of Hide and Seek can involve a group of preschoolers for long periods of time as they seek new and better places to hide.

Peek-a-boo is such a magical game, you won't be surprised to see it popping up everywhere in children's books and music. Take advantage of this and use it as often as you can. Have fun with the following suggestions.

READINGS

Where's Spot? by Eric Hill (Putnam Publishing Group)

It's time for Spot's supper, but his mommy, Sally, cannot find him. The reader helps find Spot as he lifts flaps to peek under various potential hiding places. Children delight in these manipulative books and adore Spot.

Some of the other Spot books include ***Spot's Birthday Party, Spot's First Walk, Spot's First Christmas, Spot Goes To School, Spot Goes To The Beach, Spot Goes To The Circus, Spot's First Easter***, and ***Spot Goes To The Farm.***

William, Where Are You? by Mordicai Gerstein (Crown)

It's almost bedtime, and William's mother and father can not find him. The reader goes on a William hunt, too, by opening fold-out pages to try to find him before bedtime. Another enjoyable fold-out book by this author is ***Roll Over.***

Dear Zoo by Rod Campbell (Macmillan; pb Penguin)

A little boy writes to the zoo and asks them to send him a pet, but each one they send has something wrong with it. The reader helps the little boy open each crate as the animals arrive, and then is delighted when the boy gets the perfect pet in the end. Other good manipulative books by Rod Campbell include ***Buster's Morning*** and ***Buster's Afternoon.***

There are many good manipulative books on the market now. Some other notable ones to look for are **Are You There, Bear?** (Greenwillow), **Better Move On, Frog** (Watts), **Is Anyone Home?** (Greenwillow), and **My Book** (Watts), all by Ron Maris; and **Anno's Peekaboo** (Philomel Books) by Mitsumasa Anno. Look for others, too.

RECITINGS

PEEK-A-BOO SONG
(Sung to "Frère Jacques")

Peek-a-boo, peek-a-boo,
I see you, I see you,
I see your little nose,
I see your ten toes,
I see you. Peek-a-boo!

Peek-a-boo, peek-a-boo,
I see you, I see you,
I see your curly hair,
I see your skin so fair,
I see you. Peek-a-boo!

Peek-a-boo, peek-a-boo,
I see you, I see you,
I see your eyes of blue,
I see your smile, too.
I see you. Peek-a-boo!

HIDE AND SEEK
(Sung to "Pop! Goes The Weasel")

All around my great big house,
We hide in special places.
My mom counts ten, then looks for us.
Pop! Out come our faces!

We know we're supposed to stay in our spots
Until Mom finds us first.
But we're so excited, we can't stay hidden, so,
Pop! Out we burst!

RECIPES

PEEK-A-BOO SANDWICHES
1. Mix together 1 can of tuna fish and mayonnaise, sweet pickle relish, and spices to taste (such as celery seed and/or dill).
2. Stuff pocket bread (pita) with the tuna mixture, shredded cheese, lettuce, sprouts, chopped tomato, and other favorite sandwich ingredients.
3. Close the pocket up, and then have your child peek into the sandwich to see what a delicious treat she's in for!

PEEK-A-BOO SALAD
1. Line a 1-½ quart bowl with 1 cup torn lettuce.
2. Spread 2 cups fruit, either canned or fresh, onto the lettuce.
3. Cover the fruit with one more cup of torn lettuce.
4. Mix one cup cream-style cottage cheese with 1 tablespoon of jam in the flavor of your choice. Spread this mixture over the lettuce. Use a rubber scraper to spread it so it covers all the lettuce. Cover with plastic wrap and chill for several hours.
5. Serve with a large spoon, and let your child peek into the bowl to try to figure out the surprise ingredient.

ACTIVITIES

PEEK-A-BOO VARIATIONS

Certainly everyone knows how to play peek-a-boo, but so many variations are possible that you might like to try some different ways.

■ Cover your face or your child's face with your hands; remove quickly and say, "Peek-a-boo!"

■ Cover your face and open your fingers slowly fan-style.

■ Hide behind a piece of furniture, pop out, and say, "Peek-a-boo".

■ Hide behind the newspaper, pull it down, then say, "Peek-a-boo"!

■ Attach fabric to a mirror and let the child play Peek-a-boo with himself.

■ Hide under a blanket, pop out, and say, "Peek-a-boo"!

HIDE AND SEEK VARIATIONS

■ Use only one room to hide in.

■ Use any room in the house to hide in.

■ Hide objects instead of people.

■ Set up a treasure hunt with picture clues to find what is hidden.

■ Change the method of "counting"— say the alphabet, sing a song, or recite a poem instead of counting while your child hides.

PEEK-A-BOO PICTURE

Have your child draw a picture, or use a photograph or magazine picture. Glue it to a piece of oaktag. Staple a covering flap to only one side. Have your child play peek-a-boo with the picture.

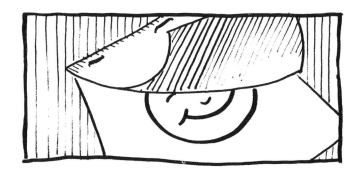

PEEK-A-BOO BOOK

Follow the procedure for a Peek-a-boo Picture, and make a series of them to compile into a simple book. If you use photographs of your family members, for example, call it "My Peek-a-boo Family," and have a page for each member of the family.

Thanksgiving Day

Over the river and through the woods
To Grandmother's house we go.

What does Thanksgiving mean to a child? If you are familiar with the rest of the lyrics to the song "Over the River," you have one poet's opinion. "...[N]ow Grandmother's face I spy. Hurray for the fun—is the pudding done? Hurray for the pumpkin pie." These lyrics suggest Thanksgiving means gathering with loved ones, playing with each other, enjoying each other's company, and having delicious treats to eat—in three simple words: family, fun, and food. These are three pretty basic things for which to be thankful.

We're always reminding our children to say "thank you." How many times have you heard yourself reminding your child to say thank you when someone compliments him or helps him or gives him something? But Thanksgiving Day goes deeper than merely saying thank you for things given or deeds done. Delve a little deeper with your child in preparing for Thanksgiving this year, and see what you and your child can discover as you take time out to be thankful together.

READINGS

Over the River and Through the Woods by Lydia Maria Child (Putnam Publishing Group)

Lovely illustrations have been added to the familiar lyrics of this seasonal song to make a special picture book.

A Charlie Brown Thanksgiving by Charles M. Schultz (Random House)

Charlie Brown gets into his usual predicaments in this story about some children who learn the meaning of sharing and giving thanks. This story can be seen on television—look for it during the holiday season and point out some of the things you and your child saw in the book to make a comparison.

It's Thanksgiving by Jack Prelutsky (Greenwillow; pb Scholastic)

This is a collection of short poems, all dealing with various aspects of Thanksgiving. Some of the titles include "If Turkeys Thought," "The Wishbone," "Gobble, Gobble," and "It's Happy Thanksgiving."

RECITINGS

WE ARE THANKFUL
(Sung to "Frère Jacques")

We are thankful, we are thankful,
For so much, for so much.
On Thanksgiving Day
You can hear us say,
Thank you, thank you.

We are thankful, we are thankful,
For food and drink, for food and drink.
On Thanksgiving Day
You can hear us say,
Thank you, thank you.

We are thankful, we are thankful,
For books to read, for books to read.
On Thanksgiving Day
You can hear us say,
Thank you, thank you.

Elicit other ideas from your child of things to be thankful for, and continue the song.

GOBBLE, GOBBLE
(Sung to "Row, Row, Row Your Boat")

A turkey is a funny bird,
His head goes wobble, wobble.
And he knows just one word,
Gobble, gobble, gobble!

RECIPES

THANKSGIVING CORNBREAD

Corn was a gift from the Indians to the Pilgrims. They taught the Pilgrims how to grow corn, which became one of their most important staples. Make some cornbread with your child to enjoy as part of your Thanksgiving feast.

1. Heat oven to 400°.
2. In an 8" or 9" square baking pan, melt ¼ cup butter or margarine in the oven. Tilt the pan to coat the bottom of the pan evenly.
3. Combine 1 cup cornmeal, 1 cup flour, 1 tablespoon sugar, 4 teaspoons baking powder, and ¼ teaspoon salt.
4. Add melted butter from pan, 1 egg, and 1 cup milk. Mix just till blended. Pour into hot pan.
5. Bake 20–25 minutes or until golden brown.

CRANBERRY-ORANGE RELISH

This easy relish goes well with turkey.

1. Cut 2 washed oranges into eight pieces each and remove all seeds. (Leave the peel on.)
2. Put these orange sections and 4 cups washed cranberries into food processor. Chop until desired consistency. Add sugar to taste.
3. Store in refrigerator for up to 2 weeks.

ACTIVITIES

THANKFUL TURKEYS

Help your child list some of the things for which he is thankful by using his hands. Cover his hands with finger paint and make two hand prints on construction paper. Once the paint has dried, add little legs at the wrists of each hand and eyes and beaks on the thumb areas with crayon. Help your child come up with eight things he's thankful for, and then you write one on each of the eight turkey-feather fingers.

THANKSGIVING MURAL

Another project you can do with finger-painted hands is to make a Thanksgiving mural with lots of turkeys strutting around the picture. Begin by having your child make several hand prints on a large piece of paper. After drying time, decorate the turkeys, and add the remaining scenery you want—perhaps some Pilgrims, Indians, trees, houses, and gardens.

TURKEY FOOTPRINTS

Use masking tape indoors or chalk outdoors to make turkey footprints on the ground. (Simply make patterns of three little straight lines with the middle one slightly ahead of the other two.) Put on some "strutting music," such as "Turkey in the Straw," and have your child strut around the house or yard like a turkey.

TANGERINE TURKEYS

Use a tangerine for the turkey's body. Insert four toothpicks as legs (you need four so it will stand up), one red pipe cleaner curled at one end as the neck and head, and fancy colored toothpicks with curly fringe (the kind for hors d'oeuvres) for tail feathers, and you have a tangerine turkey. Make one for each person who'll share your Thanksgiving meal.

Fears and Tears

Tommy's fears and Mary's tears
Will make them old before their years.

Something that causes fears and tears in every child at one time or another is separation anxiety. Separation anxiety is as inevitable as teething. The degree to which it will "hurt" varies from child to child, but you can be sure you will be going through some periods of anxiety. The idea of spending any time away from mommy or daddy breaks the emotional security the child has felt. Seeing mommy or daddy leave frightens the child, usually because he fears he'll never see them again.

It is difficult for parent as well as child, but there are things you can do to help your child understand the concept of going away and coming back. Things as simple as peek-a-boo games and hide-and-seek will show your little one that people can go—and will return. Below are more ideas to ease you through separation anxiety.

READINGS

Mommy, Where Are You? by Harriet Ziefert (pb Puffin)

Little Hippo looks in many places to find his mommy. The reader helps Hippo look and find as she lifts the flaps provided in this book. Other lift-the-flap books by the same author that are helpful in exploring going away/coming back are ***Daddy, Can You Play With Me?*** and ***Don't Cry, Baby Sam.***

Come Play With Us by Anne Sibley O'Brien (Holt, Rinehart & Winston)

Rachel's father leaves her at day care, and she is very sad when he goes. But she keeps busy and happy, and is even happier when he comes back to pick her up at the end of the day. This board book is another simply written, very comforting book.

You Go Away by Dorothy Corey (Albert Whitman & Co.)

With few words and clear pictures, this book shows situations, from a playful toss in the air to a long vacation, where children and parents are separated and reunited.

Whose Mouse Are You? by Robert Kraus (Macmillan)

Mouse is all alone; his mother is inside a cat, his father is in a trap, his sister is far from home, and he doesn't have a brother. But he does something about it. This is a satisfying story for children, as it shows Mouse in control by the end of the story.

RECITINGS

WHERE IS MOMMY?
(Sung to "Where is Thumbkin?")

Where is Mommy, where is Mommy?
She's at work, she's at work.
She's working to make money,
To buy things for her honeys.
She'll be home soon,
She'll be home soon.

Where is Daddy, where is Daddy?
At the store, at the store.
He went to buy some food,
To feed your brother and you.
He'll be home soon,
He'll be home soon.

MY PARENTS JUST LEFT
(Sung to "My Bonnie Lies Over the Ocean")

My parents just went out to dinner,
My babysitter's here with me.
She's making my favorite supper,
But I don't feel very hungry.

Bring back, bring back,
Oh, bring back my parents to me, to me.
Bring back, bring back,
Oh, bring back my parents to me.

My parents just left for the movies,
My grandparents are here with me.
I know that my mom and dad love me,
But why they go out, I don't see.

Bring back, bring back,
Oh, bring back my parents to me, to me.
Bring back, bring back,
Oh, bring back my parents to me.

My parents just went to a meeting,
Another night here without them.
I guess it's OK 'cause I know now
They will always come back again.

They'll be back, be back,
My parents will be back real soon, real soon.
They'll be back, be back,
I know they'll be back very soon.

RECIPES

YOYO COOKIES

Yoyos are toys that come back every time. Make some yoyo cookies, and talk about how you always come back, too!

1. Preheat oven to 400°.

2. Cream together ½ cup margarine and ½ cup sugar. Add 1 egg, and mix in well.

3. In another bowl, stir together 2 cups flour, ½ cup unsweetened cocoa powder, ½ teaspoon baking soda, ½ teaspoon baking powder, and a pinch of salt. Add half of this mixture to the margarine mixture and beat well.

4. Beat in 1⅓ cups buttermilk, and then the remaining flour.

5. Drop dough by rounded teaspoons about 3" apart on greased cookie sheets. Bake for 7–9 minutes.

6. While the cookies are cooling, make a batch of your favorite frosting. When cookies are cooled, spread a teaspoon of frosting on the flat side of half of the cookies. Place the remaining cookies, rounded side up, on top of the frosting. There you have cookies that look like yoyos.

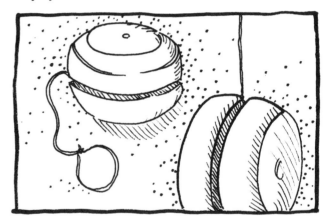

FOOD BALLS

Balls, too, can go away and can come back. Although these food balls won't bounce back to you, try to make the connection that just as balls can be rolled away and rolled back or bounced and caught again, so you will come back after you've left.

There are many foods whose natural shape is round—oranges, apples, peaches, plums, melons, tomatoes, to name just a few. Roll them back and forth to each other, perhaps across the table, and then enjoy one of them for a snack.

You can make balls from other foods using a melon-baller. Cut balls out of watermelon, cantaloupe, honeydew, or other soft-fleshed fruit.

You can make peanut butter balls. Mix 1 cup of peanut butter, ½ cup wheat germ, and ½ cup non-fat dry milk powder. Mix well. Take about a teaspoonful of the mixture and roll it into a ball between the palms of your hands. Make as many as you and your child wish, roll them around your plates, and when you're finished playing with them, munch them up for a snack.

ACTIVITIES

GOING AWAY/COMING BACK

Brainstorm with your child going away/coming back situations and role play them. Some might be mom or dad going to work, dad or mom going shopping, brother or sister going to school, hide-and-seek, peek-a-boo, vacations, going to daycare or nursery school, mom in the shower, dad in another room, waving to cars that go by or the mailman or the neighbors. You could walk outside with the child watching from the window, wave, and come back in. The more you practice going away and coming back, the more your child will understand the concept. Start simply and for very short periods, then gradually build up.

BACK TO BACK

Stand back to back with your child. On the count of three, each of you will walk a certain number of steps away from each other. When you get to the number you decided on, you will both turn around and rush back into each other's arms. Begin with a low number, perhaps only three steps away, and eventually work up to a higher number where you might even end up in different rooms before getting to rush back to each other.

HOMEMADE YOYO

This very simple yoyo will help demonstrate the concept of going away/coming back. Blow up a balloon and tie the neck. Take a piece of elastic or a long rubber band and attach it to the balloon's neck. While holding the elastic in your hand, punch the balloon away from you and see it come bouncing back from the pull of the elastic.

GOODBYE RITUAL

Sometimes children feel more comfortable when there is a set routine or ritual performed every time you leave. Just as with bedtime rituals, the child feels more in control when she knows what is going to happen next. Think up a ritual that will work for you and your child—perhaps singing a song together or exchanging a special hug and kiss or having your child bring you your pocketbook or coat. Whatever you decide together will be appropriate.

Chapter Twelve

DECEMBER
Holiday Treasures

The treasures of Christmas and Hanukkah are tough to surpass, and December is surely a favorite time of year for children. There is much work for everyone to do in preparation for these celebrations, and the more your child can participate, the more meaningful they will be. This chapter offers suggestions on how to involve your child with everything from shopping to decorating—without losing your sanity. Read on and you'll find holiday treasures for you and your toddler to share.

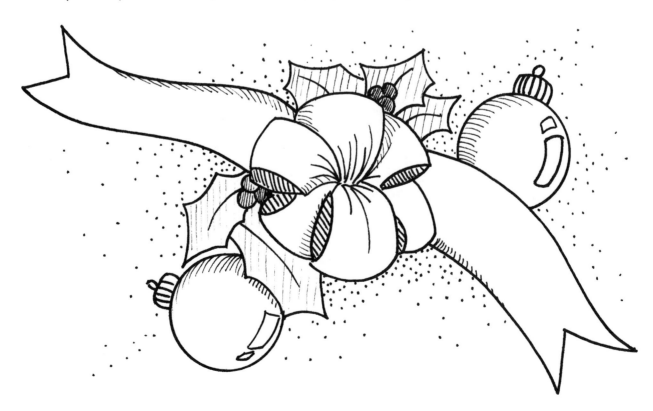

FIRST WEEK

To Market, To Market

To market, to market to buy a fat pig;
Home again, home again, jiggety jig.

December is the busiest shopping time of the year. If you're a store owner, you meet the season with great enthusiasm and anticipation; if you are a consumer, you meet it with lists and charge cards in hand; if you are a parent of young children, you'd best meet the season with a smile on your face and Tylenol in your hand! Shopping with young children, no matter what time of year, can be stressful and unpleasant for all involved. Playing hide-and-seek among the circular clothes racks, checking the quality and temperature of every water fountain in the mall, and seeing how many stuffed animals you can hold at one time are not the goals most parents have in mind when they set out to get some shopping done. But shopping doesn't have to be all work and no play, nor does it *have* to be stressful and unpleasant. With some forethought, special snacks, planned distractions, and a positive attitude, this year's holiday shopping can actually be enjoyable for both of you.

READINGS	RECITINGS

READINGS

Going Shopping by Sarah Garland (Atlantic Monthly Press)

   Comical drawings and simple words lead you on a shopping trip a mom takes with her toddler and baby.

The Shopping Basket by John Burningham (Harper Junior Books)

   This is a simple story about shopping with little ones along.

Shopping Trip by Helen Oxenbury (Dial Press)

   This board book shows an absolutely exhausting shopping trip with mother and young children. It is so popular because it is funny and true.

RECITINGS

A SHOPPING WE WILL GO
(Sung to "The Farmer in the Dell")

A shopping we will go,
A shopping we will go,
Heigh-ho, the derry-o,
A shopping we will go.

We'll all hold hands like so,
We'll all hold hands like so,
Heigh-ho, the derry-o,
We'll all hold hands like so.

We'll all help shop, we know,
We'll all help shop, we know,
Heigh-ho, the derry-o,
We'll all help shop, we know.

We'll listen and smile just so,
We'll listen and smile just so,
Heigh-ho, the derry-o,
We'll listen and smile just so.

GO ROUND AND ROUND
(Sung to "Go Round and Round the Village")

Go round and round the grocery,
Go round and round the grocery,
Go round and round the grocery,
To see what we should buy.

Let's buy some milk and butter,
Some lettuce and cucumbers,
Some chicken for our supper,
And maybe some pumpkin pie.

Go round and round the mall,
Go round and round the mall,
Go round and round the mall,
To see what we should buy.

Let's buy a book for Mary,
A shirt for Uncle Harry,
A tape for brother, Larry,
"Well done," says Mom with pride.

RECIPES

Make the following recipes to take along on your shopping expeditions and pull out whenever you need them.

SHOPPING PRETZELS
Crunchy and long-lasting!
1. Preheat oven to 425°.
2. Dissolve 1 tablespoon yeast in ½ cup warm water. Add 1 teaspoon honey and 1 teaspoon salt.
3. Add 1 cup flour and ⅓ cup wheat germ. Knead.
4. Shape into pretzel shapes (or any other shape you and your child wish). Brush with beaten egg. Sprinkle with sesame seeds.
5. Bake for 10 minutes.

ALL–IN–ONE–BITE APPLE

No mess and so tasty! Scoop out the core and seeds of an apple. Mix together 1 tablespoon peanut butter and 1 tablespoon granola (or nut/dried fruit mixture). Stuff the apple with this mixture, wrap in foil and you've got an apple ready to go.

You can also do the same thing with bananas. Cut a banana in half, spread the peanut-butter mixture in between the two layers, put the banana back together, put it back inside the skin and you've got a banana ready to go!

ACTIVITIES

Different things work with different children—and you know your child best—but try some of these on your next shopping excursion and see if they make the trip go more smoothly.

SHOPPING GAMES

Turning things into games can make life more pleasant, so why not make a game out of shopping?

■ Follow the Leader—Have your children follow you as you walk up and down the aisles and around the various stores. Make it interesting by walking in different ways: fast, slow, hopping, skipping, weaving side-to-side, or whatever else you'd like to try.

■ Simon Says—Especially fun when grocery shopping. Give commands such as, "Simon says pick up two Macintosh apples" or "Simon says do *this*" (and you pick up an item you want her to select, too.)

■ Crazy Rides—For stroller and shopping cart rides, drive the "vehicle" in a "crazy" manner, weaving back and forth, going faster, then slower, and varying the speed to give the child a changing ride.

SHOPPING MUSIC

Use music to help you through the shopping trip.

Pick out some of your favorite songs to sing together as you shop.

■ Name that Tune—Whistle, hum, or "la-la" a familiar song and let your child guess what the song is.

■ Make up your own lyrics to an old familiar tune and sing it together. For example, if you are Christmas shopping for a gift for Dede, sing to the tune of "Pop! Goes the Weasel": "All around the shopping mall, We're shopping for Dede. How about some gold earrings? Yep! That was easy!"

SHOPPING LISTS

Make lists ahead of time not only for yourself but also for your child. If you're grocery shopping, draw pictures of two or three items he can easily recognize and reach; those can be his responsibilities to get. If you are shopping at places other than grocery stores, pictures of some things to find but not necessarily to buy would be more appropriate.

Christmas Is Coming

Christmas is coming, the geese are getting fat,
Please to put a penny in an old man's hat;
If you haven't got a penny, a ha'penny will do,
If you haven't got a ha'penny, God bless you.

Christmas is coming! You can see, hear, smell, taste, and feel the signs of it everywhere. Store fronts, evergreen trees, lamp posts, and living room windows all take on a festive look as they're adorned for the holiday. Christmas music is on the radio and television, as well as being sung by carolers and choirs. The delicious aromas of special Christmas baking promise tasty delights as we get ready to treat ourselves to some of these once-a-year confections. Even our sense of touch gets involved in the Christmas spirit as we decorate our trees with tinsel, garlands, and lights, and feel their various textures.

Yes, Christmas is a holiday in which people can get totally involved. Use all of your five senses to explore this magical season with your child.

READINGS

Reading with you child always makes use of the senses of sight and hearing, but in some of these books, you'll be using all five of your senses to bring the season of Christmas right into your child's little hands.

It Feels Like Christmas! A Book of Surprises to Touch, See and Sniff illustrated by Denise Fleming (Random)

This Christmas book is a treat for little hands to hold. Touch a velvety bow, sniff an evergreen branch, and see some of the wonderful sights of Christmas in this sturdy book.

Santa's Beard is Soft and Warm by Bob Ottum and JoAnn Wood (Golden Press)

Like the one above, this is another hands-on Christmas book your little one will have fun with.

Spot's First Christmas by Eric Hill (G.P. Putnam's Sons)

It's Spot's first Christmas, and the reader is treated to the many special things in Spot's home as he and his mommy get ready for the holiday. The book has flaps for the child to lift.

Other books worth mentioning include ***The Sweet Smell of Christmas*** by Patricia Scarry (Western Publishing Co.), ***Christmas Time in New York City*** by Roxie Munro (Putnam Publishing Group), and ***Merry Christmas, Mom and Dad*** by Mercer Mayer (Golden Books).

RECITINGS

FIVE DAYS IN DECEMBER
(Sung to "The Twelve Days of Christmas")

On the first day of December,
My mommy said to me,
"Let's shop for our family."

On the sixth day of December,
My mommy said to me,
"Help me wrap the presents, please."

On the twelfth day of December,
My mommy said to me,
"Let's bake some yummy cookies."

On the eighteenth day of December,
My mommy said to me,
"Let's decorate the house and our tree."

On the twenty-fourth day of December,
My mommy said to me,
"Let's sing carols and be happy."

You may wish to simplify this song by just using first, second, third, fourth, and fifth days of December instead of the more complicated numbers.

WHERE IS CHRISTMAS?
(Sung to "Where Is Thumbkin?")

Where is Christmas, where is Christmas?
Here is is, here it is.
It's in the Christmas lights,
I see glowing so bright,
Here it is, here it is.

Where is Christmas, where is Christmas?
Here it is, here it is.
It's in the kitchen breeze,
I smell from the cookies,
Here it is, here it is.

Where is Christmas, where is Christmas?
Here it is, here it is.
It's in the wrappings there,
Of the gifts we have prepared,
Here it is, here it is.

Where is Christmas, where is Christmas?
Here is it, here it is.
It's in the lovely songs,
I hear sung all day long,
Here it is, here it is.

Where is Christmas, where is Christmas?
Here it is, here it is.
It's in the Christmas food,
I eat that is so good,
Here it is, here it is.

Where is Christmas, where is Christmas?
Here it is, here it is.
It's in the Christmas touch,
I love so very much,
Here it is, here it is.

Other special listening treats for the holiday season are the many beautiful Christmas albums available in libraries and stores. Everyone from Raffi to Pavarotti has recorded holiday music. Enjoy your favorites, and sing along with your child. Add home-made instruments such as drums and jingle bells if you wish.

RECIPES

You no doubt have many favorite recipes you can make with or for your child at this time of the year. Here are two more that are treats for both mouths *and* noses—both are especially fragrant.

WHOLE–WHEAT GINGERBREAD PEOPLE

1. In a large mixing bowl, beat 1 cup margarine, and then add ½ cup brown sugar. Beat till fluffy.

2. Add 1 egg, ⅓ cup light molasses, 1 tablespoon finely shredded orange peel, and 2 tablespoons orange juice. Beat well.

3. Mix together 3 cups white flour, 1 cup whole wheat flour, 2 teaspoons cinnamon, 1 teaspoon ginger, ½ teaspoon cloves, ½ teaspoon baking soda, and ¼ teaspoon salt. Stir into the margarine mixture. Cover and chill in the refrigerator till firm enough to roll out.

4. Turn oven to 375°. Divide the dough in half. Chill one half. On a lightly-floured surface, roll out the other half so it's ¼ inch thick. Cut with cookie cutters. Place 1" apart on un-greased cookie sheets. Repeat with remaining dough.

5. Bake 8–10 minutes or till edges are firm. Cool 1 minute. With pancake turner lift onto cooling rack.

ICING

Mix one 8-ounce package of cream cheese with 2–3 tablespoons honey. Pipe icing onto cooled cookies. Decorate with raisins, apricots and sunflower seeds. Store in refrigerator. Makes 24 cookies.

An easy way to pipe icing: Half-fill a heavy plastic sandwich bag with the icing. With scissors, snip the very tip off one corner. Roll up the empty part of the bag and squeeze the icing out of the small hole.

HOME–MADE WASSAIL

Heating this mixture on the stove not only improves its taste but also fills the whole house with its heavenly aroma.

Combine equal portions of unsweetened apple juice (or cider), cranberry juice, and orange juice. Add several cinnamon sticks and simmer for about 10 minutes.

ACTIVITIES

FEELING CHRISTMAS

This first activity involves all five senses. Before you read *It Feels Like Christmas* to your child, gather the various items mentioned in the book so you and your child can read and listen to the story (using the senses of sight and hearing) and then go on to experience all the things mentioned in the book.

HEARING CHRISTMAS

Whistle, hum, or play on the piano some Christmas carols for your child to identify. Begin with only the simplest and continue until your child can guess correctly. If he's doing well with this game, see if he can guess a song after hearing only ten notes, or maybe even fewer.

SEEING CHRISTMAS

Go for early evening rides or walks around the neighborhood at different times during the holiday season. The first time you go might be the first week in December. You can count how many houses have Christmas lights. When you go again, perhaps the next week, see how many more people have put out their Christmas lights. Help your child notice all the changes—mailbox decorations, people carry-ing packages, Christmas trees seen through windows. You may wish to keep a picture chart, the most simple type of graph, to show the changes.

Hanukkah

I have a little dreidel,
I made it out of clay.
And when it's dry and ready,
My dreidel I will play.
Dreidel, dreidel, dreidel,
I made it out of clay.
Dreidel, dreidel, dreidel,
My dreidel I will play.

Lighting candles for eight consecutive nights, giving small gifts, and playing the dreidel game are some of the traditions Jewish people enjoy during their holiday of Hanukkah. Although Hanukkah, or the Feast of Lights, is not a major Jewish holiday, it is celebrated in December by most Jewish families. It is a time of joy and thanks as they remember an occasion when the Jewish people were freed from religious oppression. Just as every holiday is celebrated according to each family's own unique flavors and traditions, so is Hanukkah. (It even is *spelled* three different ways in English: Chanukah, Hanukah and Hanukkah!)

Whether you celebrate Hanukkah with your family, have friends who do, or just want to learn more about this joyous holiday, the activities below will help you do so.

READINGS

Rainbow Candles: A Chanukah Counting Book by Myra Shostak (Kar-Ben Copies, Inc.)

Number fun found in the traditions of Chanukah make this colorful board book a good choice for your little one.

My First Chanukah by Tomie dePaola (G.P. Putnam's Sons)

When a child is first beginning to recognize the symbols of this holiday—such as the dreidel, the menorah, and latkes—this is the perfect board book.

The Eight Nights: A Chanukah Counting Book by Jane Bearman (pb UAHC Press)

This holiday book has a lively rhyme for each of the eight candles that are to be lighted. Wonderful full-color graphics show some of the delights of Chanukah, and there are even the lyrics of two songs included.

RECITINGS

ONE LITTLE, TWO LITTLE, THREE LITTLE CANDLES
(Sung to "Ten Little Indians")

One little, two little, three little candles,
Four little, five little, six little candles,
Seven and eight little candles,
On my menorah.

Eight little, seven little, six little candles,
Five little, four little, three little candles,
Two and one little candle,
On my menorah.

HANUKKAH

Let's shine up the menorah,
Let's make some special food.
Let's play games and give gifts,
Let's have fun and be good.

These are the ways we'll celebrate
Hanukkah this year.
With friends and relatives
Who are so very dear.

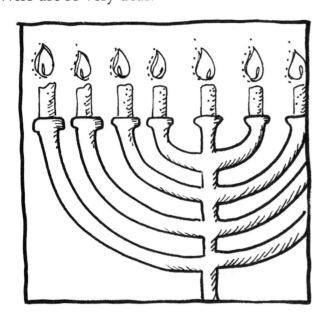

RECIPES

LATKES (POTATO PANCAKES)

1. Beat 2 eggs. Add 3 cups grated, drained potatoes, 4 tablespoons grated onion, ½ teaspoon salt, ⅛ teaspoon pepper, and 2 tablespoons cracker or matzo meal.

2. Heat ¼ cup butter in frying pan. Drop potato mixture in by tablespoons. Fry until browned on both sides.

3. Serve hot. Top with applesauce or sour cream.

DREIDEL COOKIES

A dreidel is a square-sided top used in a popular Hanukkah game. Make your favorite recipe for sugar cut-out cookies. Then use a dreidel cookie cutter or draw a dreidel on cardboard, cut it out, then use it as a pattern to cut around the dough. Decorate the cookies with frosting.

ACTIVITIES

COUNTING GAME

As there are eight days of Hanukkah—eight days of gift giving and eight days of candle lighting—counting games are appropriate at this time. Have your child count the candles in the menorah with you. Lay out eight items and encourage your child to pick up one, then two, then three of them. Make up singing games using the numbers one to eight. Put the numbers in a hopscotch diagram on the floor using masking tape, and jump from one number to the next. There are lots of ways to have fun with numbers.

EGG CARTON MENORAH

Make a simple menorah that your child can "light" each of the eight days of the holiday. Break off and discard four sections of an empty egg carton. Turn the remaining eight sections face down. Poke a small hole in each, and insert a real or pretend candle in each one. Color or decorate as you wish.

HANUKKAH CHAIN

Cut 2" x 6" strips from blue and white construction paper. Glue the ends of one strip together to make a loop for the first link. Glue the ends of a second strip together after having passed it through the first link. Alternating colors, make as many links as there are days left of the holiday—or if you've gotten a good head start, you can begin on December 1st and make a link for each day until Hanukkah begins. Have your child cut a link off each day until the chain is gone.

Christmas Comes But Once a Year

Christmas comes but once a year,
And when it comes it brings good cheer.

"Christmas comes but once a year." Are you glad or sorry? When you can count the hours left until Christmas, you might feel excitement and anticipation—or panic and pressure. It depends on how far along in your preparations you happen to be. No matter how you're feeling at this late date, you can be sure that in your child's view, Christmas is just as thrilling as ever. Christmas is a glorious time when seen through the eyes of a child, and that's how all people, young and old, should see it. Find some spare moments in these last few days before Christmas to read a tender Christmas story, play a special Christmas game, and share some loving closeness with your child.

READINGS

Max's Christmas by Rosemary Wells (Dial Books for Young Readers)

Max wants to stay up to see Santa, but his sister, Ruby, says no. Even though she seems to have an answer to every question Max asks, Max surprises Ruby in the end with the answer he gives to her four pressing questions of him. This is another wonderful Max story that will delight all Max's fans.

Happy Christmas, Gemma by Sarah Hayes (Lothrop)

If you have a baby in your house or remember what it's like to have one there at Christmas time, you'll love this book. Gemma puts her special touch on every Christmas preparation and makes the reader laugh with delight.

Little Tree by e.e. cummings, illustrated by Deborah Kogan Ray (Crown)

Ms. Ray has added drawings equal to this beautiful and sensitive Christmas poem by e.e. cummings. It's an outstanding holiday book.

Carl's Christmas by Alexandra Day (Farrar Straus Giroux)

It's Christmas Eve, and Carl—the Rottweiler Alexandra Day created in her earlier *Good Dog, Carl*—is left to tend the baby while his master and mistress go to Christmas Eve services. The breathtaking illustrations tell the story so eloquently that no text is necessary.

RECITINGS

WE WISH YOU A MERRY CHRISTMAS

To add to the fun, make up new lyrics and movements to this traditional holiday tune.

Chorus:
We wish you a merry Christmas,
We wish you a merry Christmas,
We wish you a merry Christmas
And a happy New Year.

Let's all do a little jumping,
Let's all do a little jumping,
Let's all do a little jumping
And spread Christmas cheer.

Chorus

Let's all do a little clapping, *etc.*
Let's all do a little hopping, *etc.*
Let's all do a little skipping, *etc.*

CHRISTMAS IS COMING

All around my house I can see
That Christmas Day is coming.
The tree is up, the presents are wrapped,
And I've even hung up my stocking.

I can hear the church bells ring,
And Christmas carolers singing
All is ready—just one more day,
How I love this Christmas feeling!

RECIPES

Prepare a special Christmas breakfast of nutritious munching foods. A sit-down breakfast isn't very popular or very practical when gifts are waiting to be opened.

FRUIT–FULL CHRISTMAS TREE

1. Begin with a cone-shaped piece of styrofoam. Choose your family's favorite fruits and cut bite-size pieces of them. Grapes, orange pieces (perhaps mandarin oranges from a can), pineapple chunks, pear chunks, and bananas would all be fine.

2. Stick one piece of fruit on the end of a toothpick and insert the other end of the toothpick into the styrofoam cone, beginning at the bottom. Continue adding fruit, working your way up to the top of the cone.

3. Put the fruit-filled cone on a serving plate and serve as is or with a bowl of yogurt on the side as a dip. (Remember to help your child remove the toothpicks to avoid breaking and choking.)

COFFEE CAKE MUFFINS

Muffins are a good choice to serve along with the fruit-full Christmas tree. Choose your family's favorite kind (or use the recipe below), make a batch, and leave them on the table in a festive basket. Serve with butter, jams, or spreads of your liking.

1. Preheat oven to 350°.

2. Beat ½ cup oil, 2 eggs, and ⅓ cup sugar together.

3. Add 1 cup low-fat yogurt (either plain or vanilla-flavored) and 1-½ teaspoons vanilla.

4. Sift and add ½ cup whole wheat flour, ½ cup white flour, ½ teaspoon baking powder, 1 teaspoon baking soda, and ½ teaspoon cinnamon. Add ½ cup wheat germ. Beat until just mixed.

5. Pour batter into greased muffin tins, filling cups only half full. Sprinkle each with ½ teaspoon of the following mixture, and then cover with the remaining batter. Mixture: 1 tablespoon sugar, ½ teaspoon cinnamon, and 3 tablespoons chopped walnuts.

6. Bake for 25 minutes.

ACTIVITIES

Now (if you're lucky) the gifts are wrapped, the cookies are baked, the tree is decorated, and the Christmas menu is under control. With all this time on your hands, you can try some of these ideas for things to do with your little one.

SPECIAL SANTA PICTURE

Ask your child if he might like to draw a special picture for Santa. Give him free rein on what to draw, and then leave the picture with Santa's cookies and milk, perhaps with a note that tells him what your child would like him to know.

SPECIAL SANTA TAPE

Record your child singing some Christmas songs, telling a story, or just saying some of your favorite words that he says so well. You might suggest that you leave the tape for Santa to listen to, or you might just like to keep it for yourselves and add to it from time to time. Be sure to say the date onto the tape so you'll know years later just when it was made.

CHRISTMAS BREAKFAST PLACE MATS

Give your child a big piece of construction paper (red, white, or green) for herself—and another one for each member of the family, if you'd like and if she has the attention span and desire. Have her design a special place mat for Christmas morning breakfast that will help make the table look even more festive. If you'd like to save them for future use, cover the finished mats with clear contact paper.

Index

Arts and Crafts

Authors

Books

Dramatic Play

Games

Recipes

Science

Special Events

Storytelling

Other books of interest from
August House Publishers

Time Out Together
by Jan Brennan
A month-by-month guide to activities to enjoy with children ages four to nine.
The ideas are original, uncomplicated, and make use of materials everyone has on hand.
pb $12.95 • ISBN 0-87483-103-2

Favorite Scary Stories of American Children
collected by Richard and Judy Dockrey Young
Favorite tales newly collected from children ages five to ten.
Shivery stories of vengeful ghosts, spooky stories of witches and spirits,
and giggly stories that turn fear to fun.
pb $8.95 • ISBN 0-87483-119-9

American Children's Folklore
by Simon J. Bronner
"Earns straight A's in the Nostalgia Test....
All the terrible beauty of childhood is here." —*Washington Post Book World*
pb $11.95 • ISBN 0-87483-068-0
pb $19.95 • ISBN 0-87483-069-9 • Annotated edition

Miss Mary Mac All Dressed in Black
by Scott E. Hastings, Jr.
Tongue twisters, jump-rope rhymes, and other children's lore from New England.
"With respectful good cheer, Hastings has evoked and preserved
a precious lode of the region's cultural riches." —*The Boston Globe*
pb $8.95 • ISBN 0-87483-156-3

Listening for the Crack of Dawn
by Donald Davis
Growing-up stories—funny and true, nostalgic and poignant—from storyteller Donald Davis.
"A delightful memoir—warm and bittersweet, at times humorous
and at other times heart-rending." —*Library Journal*
hb $17.95 • ISBN 0-87483-153-9
pb $9.95 • ISBN 0-87483-1130-X

Big Doc's Girl
a novel by Mary Medearis
"Warmly written in an unaffectedly musical prose, alive with real people and the
fires of living, filled with uproarious humor and dialogue that is exactly right,
this brilliantly human story lives with you long after the
last reluctantly turned page." —*The Los Angeles Times*
pb $7.95 • ISBN 0-87483-105-9

Homecoming: The Southern Family in Short Fiction
edited by Rod Lorenzen and Liz Parkhurst
Stories by Eudora Welty, Alice Walker, Larry Brown, Lee Smith, and others.
"The family secrets revealed in this collection will not only entertain, they will
remind you that your family is a fragile, precious thing." —*Southern Living*
hb $17.95 • ISBN 0-87483-112-1

August House Publishers, Inc. • P.O. Box 3223, Little Rock, AR 72203 • 1-800-284-8784